High Definition Life

High Definition Life

Going Full Throttle for Life's Best

Student Edition

Luis Palau
with Steve Halliday

Featuring a word from Stephen Baldwin

Revell
Grand Rapids, Michigan

Published by Fleming H. Revell
a division of Baker Publishing Group
P.O. Box 6287, Grand Rapids, MI 49516-6287

Printed in the United States of America

Library of Congress Cataloging-in-Publication Data
Palau, Luis, 1934–
    High definition life : going full throttle for life's best / Luis Palau and Steve Halliday.—Student ed.
        p.   cm.
    Includes bibliographical references.
    ISBN 0-8007-3053-4 (pbk.)
        1. Youth—Religious life. 2. Christian life. I. Halliday, Steve, 1957–
II. Title.
    BV4531.3.P35 2005
    248.8'3—dc22   2004021889

Published in association with the literary agency of Alive Communications, Inc., 7680 Goddard Street, Suite 200, Colorado Springs, CO 80920.

interior design by brian brunsting

CONTENTS

When I first became a Christian, I started looking for what might be out there for young believers in movies, music, and television that was relevant to the youth culture. I've always been drawn to the edgy lifestyle—in my acting roles and in my own life—and I wasn't finding much in the "Christian world" that spoke to me.

Then one night on the beach in Fort Lauderdale, I experienced a Luis Palau Festival. I'd gone there to check out some of my favorite musicians—Third Day, Pillar, tobyMac—but I also got to meet Luis and hear him share the Good News with a crowd of over 200,000 people. His message—like this book—was filled with hope, challenge, and great storytelling.

I also saw for the first time the amazing skateboard and BMX athletes that draw thousands of kids to Luis's events. These guys were "livin' it," showing young people that you really can live a life of excellence and faith. That Fort Lauderdale encounter led to a partnership with Kevin Palau and the Palau team producing extreme sports DVDs called "Livin' It," as well as a "Livin' It LIVE" skate tour that will be reaching people around the world for Christ.

Luis Palau's life and ministry have been filled with "God's best." Luis has shown me how to live at full throttle and still keep my eyes on Jesus. I pray this book will help guide you to your own amazing adventure.

INTRODUCTION
I Never Knew It Was Like That

A few days before he turned seventeen, a young man named Matt Higgins received what probably ranks as the best gift of his life: he got his sight back.

At just four years of age, Matt contracted Stevens Johnson Syndrome, a rare affliction that occurs when the body has a severe reaction to antibiotics or infection. The illness left his eyes badly damaged, and by age eight, "My vision was blurry, like looking through fog constantly," Matt said. And the fog didn't lift for nine long years.

Then, in the summer of 2003, everything changed. Matt underwent two breakthrough surgeries, scheduled three months apart, to restore his normal vision. Just one week after the second operation, Matt could read a book while holding it at arm's length; prior to his surgeries, he could read only by pressing his face right against the page and straining to make out individual words. His doctor confidently expected Matt's vision to continue to improve over the next few months.[1]

Can you imagine the thrill that Matt must be experiencing? What once looked blurry now looks sharp. What before he couldn't begin to make out, now he can see clearly. I imagine the blues look bluer, the reds look redder, and the whole world has taken on a new and exciting appearance. More than once, I'd be willing to guess, Matt has exclaimed to his friends and family, "It's amazing! I never knew it was like that."

I think such an excited reaction provides a good model for life in general. In my opinion, too many of us settle for a life in drab shades of gray when we could be enjoying it in all the brilliant colors of God's imagination. We pull in to Slim's Greasy Spoon for a burger and fries when we've been invited to Paris for a six-course meal prepared by Europe's finest chefs—all expenses paid.

That's not to say hamburgers are bad; I'd still rather have a hot sandwich (or some blurry vision) than nothing at all. But why choose a slab of fried ground beef when you can have succulent steak? Why continue to read with your eyes pressed smack against the page when you can take in the whole book and enjoy it as the author intended?

Why grab a rhinestone when you could have a diamond?

Why shoot for a consolation prize when you could win the jackpot?

Why spend a weekend in Toad Suck, Arkansas, when you could enjoy a fourteen-day cruise to Tahiti?

Why settle for a thirty-year-old black and white television set with no cable hookup when you can have a state-of-the-art widescreen plasma unit designed for HDTV? In other words, why choose

What Scripture helps you focus on choosing God's best?

Psalm 37:4 "Delight yourself in the LORD and he will give you the desires of your heart." This Scripture makes me focus on God's best, because when we diligently seek the kingdom he guides us down the right path.

Kyle Mitchell, Kutless

Too often we settle for skimming through a psalm before bed or reciting a ten-second mealtime prayer and consider that "having devotions" or "talking to God." When we give God our "good enough," that's all we can expect him to give back to us. Why not give God our best and see what he can really do?

Elizabeth Ries Jones, author and editor

Who is one person you see as living a high definition life?

When I was younger, I pretty much wanted to do everything that my older brother Jesse did. My brother got me into skateboarding and taught me all the basic tricks. Jesse turned his life over to God when he moved out of the house. God spoke to him on a park bench. He heard the Lord call his name so loudly he turned around. He was into a cult at the time. He called my parents and told them he came back to the Lord on the park bench. So my parents drove out to Colorado and got him out of the cult. Jesse now heads up GX International. It's a ministry based around skateboarding, rollerblading, BMX biking, break dancing, and choreographed dancing that tours all across the United States and around the world. He's one of my best friends. He is the best role model I could ever have. I love him.

Sierra Fellers,
skateboard champion

a low resolution existence when you can have a high definition life?

This book is not about deciding between "bad" and "good" but about choosing "best" over "good enough." It's about getting everything out of life that your Creator intended for you to have. It's about going hard after the greatest things available in this world. I want to paint a picture of the great possibilities offered to you by God when you choose the full Christian life.

Perhaps I could borrow as my "theme statement" a line written two thousand years ago by a man who knew all about choosing "best" over "good enough." In a letter to some friends in which he laid out a blueprint for successful living, the apostle Paul wrote, "Let me tell you about something else that is better than any of them!" (1 Cor. 12:31).

That's what I want to do in this book—show you "something else that is better than any of them." I'd like to take a look at ten "good" areas of life and show how something even better and more excellent is waiting for you.

Along the way we'll keep in mind a memorable statement made to a young American visiting Taiwan: "Young man, remember that your life is like a coin. You can spend it any way you want, but you can spend it only once."

My question is, how are you going to spend it? You can settle for "good enough," or you can choose "the best." The choice is yours.

The High Definition Life means choosing "best" over "good enough." It's about getting everything out of life that your Creator intended for you to have.

25 words or less

WISE WORDS

I AM FOCUSING ALL MY ENERGIES ON THIS ONE THING: FORGETTING THE PAST AND LOOKING FORWARD TO WHAT LIES AHEAD, I STRAIN TO REACH THE END OF THE RACE AND RECEIVE THE PRIZE FOR WHICH GOD, THROUGH CHRIST JESUS, IS CALLING US UP TO HEAVEN.

the apostle Paul, Philippians 3:13-14

A Lifelong Source of Thrills

Excitement or Adventure?

There's nothing like a little excitement to add some zip to your life. You know the awesome feeling: that amazing rush of adrenaline as you prepare to

- kiss the guy or girl of your dreams
- claim an unexpected, last-second victory
- meet your hero in person
- get ready for summer vacation

Jason Hale and Dixie-Marie Prickett certainly know that sweet feeling. Jason, a neurotrauma nurse, and Dixie-Marie, a kayak instructor, lived their dream summer in 2001. They spent four months kayaking, romancing, and "checking out lots of waterfalls and lots of exciting places" across the United States.

Jason said, "I love surfing a wave and 'dropping' a twenty- to thirty-foot waterfall early in the morning." He likened "dropping down" to a very fast elevator ride off the lip of a waterfall into the basin pool below.

Both admit that kayaking waterfalls involves risks. Jason has even broken his back once and is still haunted by dreams of his accident. He now strives to perfect his landing, and each time he runs a waterfall correctly, "I come up and '*Whooee*! I didn't break my back this time!' It's just awesome."[1]

Despite the risks, the excitement of white-water kayaking defines Dixie-Marie and Jason's lives.

The Many Faces of Excitement

Fortunately, excitement comes not only when we avoid breaking our backs but in a wild variety of shapes and flavors.

Do a search for "adrenaline rush" in a popular electronic encyclopedia, and up pops a picture of a pair of skydivers. The caption reads, "Because of the sensation of leaping into the air and free-falling some distance before opening their parachutes, skydivers usually experience a rush of adrenaline and then a peaceful sense of well-being."[2]

Turn to the Internet and you can find not only skydiving but also bungee jumping, tornado chasing, and running with the bulls in Pamplona, Spain.

The Travel Channel once aired a program called "101 Things You Should Do to Have a Full Life"—suggestions like attending space camp or taking a deep-sea voyage to the *Titanic*.

The Physiology of Excitement

Why do we crave excitement? Why do we want to spend outrageous amounts of money and time in its wild pursuit? Mostly because of the way it makes us feel.

The human body responds to excitement very much like it reacts to stress. When we get excited, the autonomic nervous system directs the adrenal glands to secrete epinephrine (also called adrenaline) and norepinephrine into the blood stream, causing the heart to beat more rapidly, blood pressure to rise, breathing to accelerate, the pupils to dilate, perspiration to increase, and increased amounts of blood to flow to the brain and muscles from the internal organs and skin.

Our bodies also produce abnormally high levels of endorphins during periods of intense stress or excitement. Endorphins play a huge role in producing the feelings of ecstasy or pleasure we feel when we get excited—whether that excitement comes from earning an unexpectedly good grade, winning a close game, or getting a date with that "special someone."

Because we hunger for the intense feelings generated by excitement, more and more people are pursuing the ever-escalating thrills provided by "extreme sports." Gravity-defying tricks on skateboards, bikes, and snowboards are just some examples. Bungee jumping has its fans, and if we can't do it ourselves, we watch breathlessly as someone else takes the plunge. And these days a lot of people are opting for "adventure vacations."

Some psychologists see this fascination with extreme sports as a modern substitute for vision quests and the traditional rites of passage found in other cultures. Other experts believe such sports represent a reaction to the relative safety of modern life.

Maybe. But I think most extreme sports nuts get involved simply for the thrill of it, for the heart-pounding, blood-pumping, face-flushing adrenaline rush that leaves them with "a peaceful sense of well-being."

We're designed to enjoy things that stir up our emotions or feelings. Excitement makes us feel good, brightens our outlook, and puts a smile on our face. We're naturally drawn

Think of excitement as the acorn and adventure as the oak. Don't settle for a squirrel's treat when you can have the whole tree!

25 words or less

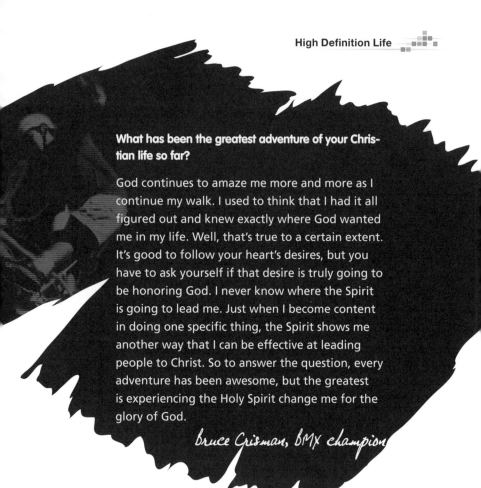

What has been the greatest adventure of your Christian life so far?

God continues to amaze me more and more as I continue my walk. I used to think that I had it all figured out and knew exactly where God wanted me in my life. Well, that's true to a certain extent. It's good to follow your heart's desires, but you have to ask yourself if that desire is truly going to be honoring God. I never know where the Spirit is going to lead me. Just when I become content in doing one specific thing, the Spirit shows me another way that I can be effective at leading people to Christ. So to answer the question, every adventure has been awesome, but the greatest is experiencing the Holy Spirit change me for the glory of God.

Bruce Crisman, BMX champion

to whatever can get us going, arouse our senses, and awaken our built-in desire for *adventure*.

Ah, adventure! The word itself suggests excitement—but also something more, something beyond, something extra. My dictionary declares adventure to be "an undertaking involving risk, unforeseeable danger, or unexpected excitement."[3] When I think of adventure, my mind fills with electrifying images of dangerous quests in exotic lands undertaken for a worthy purpose. Excitement may raise my pulse for a moment, but real adventure supplies me with a lifelong source of thrills.

In other words, excitement's good, but adventure's better.

How's It Better?

Of all possible adventures, the Christian life is the greatest. It qualifies at every point: It's exciting; it lasts a lifetime; it's rooted in a noble cause; and unexpected danger accompanies it everywhere. While earthly adventures may tempt death, the Christian life actually affects life *after* death.

Understand, I'm not talking about the bland, apathetic Christian life of too many couch potato believers in these La-Z-Boy days. I'm talking about the risk-taking kind of faith that has prompted believers throughout the centuries to sail uncharted waters, cross dangerous borders, confront powerful kings, give away fortunes, minister to the desperately sick, and eagerly offer even their lives in hazardous service to the King of Kings.

The Christian life truly is the grandest adventure of all— despite what some commentators say. Too many of them try to tone down a believer's natural enthusiasm with grim warnings. "Adventure?" they ask. "Sure. But never forget that Jesus told us, 'In the world you'll have tribulation.'" Or they say, "Don't think it's going to be easy!" Or they remind us, "Satan's just around the corner!"—as if we didn't know it. Of course, we know it perfectly well. Who's ever heard of an *easy* adventure? Overcoming obstacles and facing dangers are what *make* adventure wonderful.

We're not frightened because the devil's lurking around the next bend. Listen, he's *always* been there—and he prowls around comfortable, low-risk lives too. I say, let's deal with Satan by tapping into the power of God—that's also part of the adventure.

Real adventure, the kind offered by a full-throttle Christian life, touches the deepest part of us and opens up a world of wonder, while mere excitement makes our pulse rise for a few moments and then leaves a vacuum inside that demands an even bigger rush next time. Adventure lasts over the long haul, while excitement sticks around for about as long as the career of a reality TV loser. Excitement, as good as it is, comes in second to adventure in at least five important ways:

Excitement	Adventure
• Appetizing	• Satisfying
• Physiological	• Spiritual
• Focused inward	• Focused outward
• Event-oriented	• People-oriented
• Momentary	• Lifelong

Think of excitement as the acorn and adventure as the oak. Don't settle for a squirrel's treat when you can have the whole tree!

Appetizing vs. Satisfying

Think of excitement as an appetizer and adventure as a full-course meal. Buffalo wings or fried mozzarella sticks may taste delicious, but you wouldn't want to try to fill up on them; you need a ham dinner or an all-you-can-eat pizza buffet for that. Excitement provides spice to life, but who can live off of spices? Think of adventure as the main course, spiced up with excitement.

Unfortunately, many people mistake the sizzle for the steak. Tom Landry, former coach of the NFL's Dallas Cowboys, made exactly that error before he discovered true adventure in the middle of his celebrated life.

Landry won all-pro honors as a defensive back with the New York Giants in the 1950s, then coached the Cowboys from 1960 to 1988. He led his team to five Super Bowl appearances, winning twice. When he died on February 12, 2000, he still ranked third on the NFL's all-time win list with 270 victories.

The coach spoke briefly at one of our mission events a number of years ago. "I wanted to climb that ladder of success that's made America so great," he said. "I had great success at football at the University of Texas. We won the Sugar Bowl; we won the Orange Bowl my senior year. But each time we had the excitement of winning these games, there was something missing. I was empty and restless, and I didn't understand why that was. I thought that when you had success like that, you should be excited all the time. But that wasn't true. I thought, *Well, I just haven't reached the top.*"

After graduation Landry joined the New York Giants in the NFL, where he earned further success. His team won the world championship in 1956 against the Chicago Bears and in 1958 played against the Baltimore Colts in one of the greatest professional games ever. But again, the emptiness gnawed at him.

"I went to a friend of mine in Dallas and told him about my problem," Landry said. "I was empty and restless; I didn't understand why I wasn't getting the fulfillment I thought I should have."

His friend immediately identified the problem. He asked Landry to attend a Bible study that met in a Dallas hotel, but Landry resisted. "Heck," he explained, "I'd been to church every Sunday as long as I could remember. I knew the Christmas story and the Easter story, and I didn't think I needed any more."

But his friend finally persuaded him to go, and when Landry walked in to his first meeting, he heard the group discussing the Gospel of Matthew. Landry's ears popped wide open when he heard the words of Jesus Christ: "So I tell you, don't worry about everyday life—whether you have enough food, drink, and clothes. Doesn't life consist of more than food and clothing?" (Matt. 6:25).

And he wondered, *Could this be the adventure I've missed?*

Soon afterward, at age thirty-five, he committed his life to Jesus Christ. The next year he took over as coach of the Cowboys and immediately made it clear to players and coaches alike that he had adopted a new set of priorities: God first, family second, football third. Bob Lilly, a future all-pro lineman, had a hard time buying his new coach's priorities; he just didn't think they could work. After retiring he admitted to Landry, "You know, Coach, when you told me that, I didn't think we'd ever win a football game." Landry just smiled—easy to do when you've "had twenty years of winning," in the coach's words.

Quite an adventure—and much more satisfying than mere excitement.

God offers all of us the adventure of a lifetime through a dynamic, thrilling, unpredictable, yet satisfying journey with Jesus Christ. When I consider the life of the apostle Paul, for example, I see one of the greatest adventurers in human history.

Paul seldom knew a dull day. Because he worked to introduce as many people as possible to Jesus Christ, he never found himself bored or fighting a sense of purposelessness. Meaning filled his life. But Paul also faced danger. Listen to his own account of his exploits:

> I have worked harder, been put in jail more often, been whipped times without number, and faced death again and again. . . . Three times I was shipwrecked. Once I spent a whole night and a day adrift at sea. I have traveled many weary miles. I have faced danger from flooded rivers and from robbers. I have faced danger from my own people, the Jews, as well as from the Gentiles. I have faced danger in the cities, in the deserts, and on the stormy seas. I have lived with weariness and pain and sleepless nights. Often I have been hungry and thirsty and have gone without food. Often I have shivered with cold, without enough clothing to keep me warm . . . When I was in Damascus, the governor under King Aretas kept guards at the city gates to catch me. But I was lowered in a basket through a window in the city wall, and that's how I got away!
>
> 2 Corinthians 11:23, 25–27, 32–33

Talk about adventure! Paul's life makes the movie exploits of Indiana Jones sound like an amusement park ride (which, I've heard, they are). His friends pleaded with him not to go on one dangerous journey, but he insisted that another adventure awaited him there. He wrote to a group of friends, "My life is worth nothing unless I use it for doing the work assigned me by the Lord Jesus—the work of telling others the Good News about God's wonderful kindness and love" (Acts 20:22–24).

How could a man like that ever get bored? How could a believer with a mission that big, a passion that hot, and a God that great ever settle for mere excitement? He couldn't.

And neither should you.

Physiological vs. Spiritual

While excitement is primarily a physiological reaction to an outside stimulus—a mix of exploding endorphins, flowing adrenaline, wide eyes, and increased pulse rate—adventure leaps far beyond the physical to embrace the spiritual.

The best adventures are always connected to a noble cause or mission. The greatest adventurers crisscross the world not only for the thrills but also to accomplish a worthy purpose. Because the excitement they feel connects to a far greater objective, they enjoy a deeper, richer, and longer-lasting pleasure than those who are after only an adrenaline rush.

That's another reason the Christian life presents the best opportunities for adventure. Those who partner with God to extend his kingdom—whether they do so in the classroom, lunchroom, or locker room—know an ongoing thrill unavailable to others. It's one thing to risk your life to set a (soon-to-be-broken) record in street luge; it's quite another to risk it to bring eternal life to those who desperately need it.

When my four sons were younger and I was getting ready to travel to a dangerous part of the world, I often explained to them that I might never return from that particular trip. I felt it was my duty. Of course I didn't want to die, and I prayed privately that if it came to that, the end would come without pain. I'm a chicken like anyone else; I hope to live till I'm ninety-two. But the danger had to be faced, and in the power of Christ, it can be. The bottom line: if our Master died for us, what an honor it would be to die for him!

I almost had the honor forced on me several times.

In 1984, during a mission in the city of Arequipa, Peru, thousands of men and women had made a commitment to Jesus Christ. In South America people often give the speaker letters or notes as he walks out of the stadium, and I habitually put the pieces of paper in my pocket. When my team and I got back to the hotel on the next-to-last day of the crusade, we broke into songs of praise. As my team continued to talk and sing, I took out an envelope and slowly read a note from the Tupac Amaru—one of Peru's infamous terrorist groups. My singing stopped at the words: "You leave the country within 24 hours, you criminal, or you're going to die like a dog. You deserve the worst, you thief, you murderer, you dirty capitalist."

Immediately we gave the note to the Peruvian secret police. Their faces turned pale as they verified the note's style and seal. "Yes, this is real," they told us. "We'll have to protect you."

Talk about creepy! I couldn't sleep that night. You don't mind going to heaven when it's your time, but you don't want someone planning to send you there early.

The terrorists had ordered us to leave Peru, but we had a mission scheduled for Lima—with no safe way out of Arequipa. By car we would have to drive right through territory controlled by the terrorists. By air we had our choice of one flight in the morning or one at night. So if they wanted to get us, they could get us.

After much prayer we decided that leaving would be the most cowardly thing to do. What kind of Christian leader would I be if I quit just because I was threatened? So we stayed.

What do you think would be the ultimate adventure in your faith?

The ultimate adventure will be when I get to meet Jesus Christ face-to-face! The climax of our journey of faith is heaven—our final destination. The journey is great . . . but nothing beats what God has in store for us for all eternity.

Jose Zayas, youth evangelist

We switched to a hotel with two underground exits, left the hotel from the basement, and changed cars several times on the way to the stadium. We'd swap cars in the middle of the street—the police stopped all traffic, and we exchanged cars and scooted off a different way. And when we arrived at the stadium, nobody could talk to me.

On the last night of the campaign, police swarmed all over the place, using dogs to inspect the stadium. Of course, we knew committed terrorists could still get me. If gunmen of the past could manage to assassinate three different U.S. presidents, their modern counterparts could easily get an evangelist like me.

After our meetings ended, we snuck out; police made all the arrangements. Still, we knew the Tupac

Amaru had people everywhere. Even on the plane for Lima, I couldn't help but look at every face and wonder, *Is there a killer in here?*

During such an adventure, you realize that only the Lord can protect you. And you're grateful that he can keep you safe not only from the Tupac Amaru in Peru but from unknown enemies of all kinds.

Can serving Jesus Christ put your life at risk? It can, and it might. But what could be better than exchanging a few moments of danger for eternal dividends?

Focused Inward vs. Focused Outward

When something excites us, we can't help but get caught up in the wild emotions that overwhelm us. Our focus naturally turns inward to how we feel, how we respond to this new thrill.

Real adventure turns the focus outward without diminishing even a little your ability to enjoy events. It expands your field of vision, broadens your horizons, and enlarges your capacity for joy. And your excitement doubles when you see how your efforts make others excited too.

I don't think I have ever felt more excited than when I have seen God use my efforts to help "open up" a nation previously closed to the gospel of Jesus Christ.

I have prayed for the People's Republic of China since 1949, when the Communists took over and stories of persecuted Christians started drifting into the West. I had read the remarkable tales of Hudson Taylor, a pioneering missionary to China in the 1800s, so even as a little boy, I thought, *Someday, I'm going to go to China and preach. And when I go, I don't want to enter through any other port but Shanghai.* Why Shanghai? Because that's where Hudson Taylor crossed the border. I know, I know—a crazy, sentimental desire. Who cares what port you come in through? But to me it felt somehow meaningful.

For fifty years I continued to pray, "Lord, let me preach in Shanghai!" During that time I preached in Singapore, Hong Kong, and Taiwan—close, but not quite there. I led a mission event in Hong Kong in 1997. After giving the invitation I said, "Well, my dear Chinese, I'll see you in heaven, or I'll see you in Shanghai." I'm amazed that I actually said such a thing in public, because I knew that mainland China officials sat in the audience. But I did say it—and three years later, I found myself entering China to preach . . . in Shanghai!

The green rice paddies and modern cities of China are beautiful, but nothing could compare to the three churches I preached in at the invitation of the Shanghai Christian Council. Each church was impossibly jammed with happy people sitting tightly together, singing with full voices to Jesus Christ. I tell you, there's nothing like it!

Persecution still exists and China has a long way to go. But it seems inevitable that great changes are coming to the People's Republic of China. I say this based not only on what I saw but on my conversations with key people. I now pray even more that God would completely open up that long-closed nation.

Do you crave adventure? If so, I encourage you to look for opportunities to help open up a country to the blessings of God. Research a "closed" country, then pray daily for its government and citizens.[4] Support overseas missionaries financially—and go on a short-term missions trip yourself. God knows what thrills you and what is useful for his kingdom. Don't be afraid to ask God about what adventures he has planned for *your* life.

Event-Oriented vs. People-Oriented

When we seek excitement for its own sake, events take center stage. On the other hand, adventure involves event after eye-popping event in which people dominate. That's why the Christian life offers the greatest adventure you can imagine. What could be better than working with God in a high-stakes mission to bring salvation to people who desperately need it?

Corrie ten Boom, the late Dutch evangelist who spent time in a Nazi concentration camp, used to recite a poem I love:

> When I enter that beautiful city
> and the saints all around appear,
> I hope that someone will tell me,
> "It was you who invited me here."

It excites me when someone walks up and says, "Luis, something great has happened! For the first time in my life, I was able to lead someone to a personal relationship with Jesus Christ."

A few years ago a twenty-year-old college student approached me. "Luis," she said, "I've been a Christian for two years. I received training from your staff, became a counselor for the event, and had the privilege of leading a number of people to Christ!"

"Are you excited?" I wondered.

"Am I excited!" she exclaimed. "My question is, what am I going to do *now*? I graduate in June, and there's only one thing I want to do in life, and that's win people to Christ."

If only more of God's children would discover that kind of excitement! Of course, you don't have to attend an evangelistic event to get excited about planting seeds that may help others cross from death to eternal life. Individual Christians faithfully make the most of their opportunities all the time.

Mandy was thirteen when I met her during a youth rally at a church outside of London, England. After speaking to that group of young people, I spent several minutes alone with her talking about her eternal destiny.

Mandy told me that her father, a famous London jazz musician, and her mother, a well-known British actress, were divorced.

Touring with my band Kutless for the last four years has been the greatest adventure of my Christian life. Unfortunately I travel so much that I rarely attend church. This has caused me to really create a solid devotional relationship with Christ to remain grounded and on track. The most exciting part of the Christian adventure for me is when God "shows up" and "shows off." I think that the ultimate adventure in my life would be children—having them.

Kyle Mitchell, Kutless

They never attended church, never talked about God, and didn't even own a Bible.

Mandy said she had never heard about Jesus Christ. But when she learned that Jesus died for her sins, rose again, and was coming back to take all those who believed in him to heaven, she prayed with me and invited Jesus into her heart.

As the months passed, Mandy began to tell others what Jesus Christ had done for her. She told her family and her school friends that she knew she was going to heaven when she died.

Three years later the phone call came. I was told that Mandy had gone on a date three days before her sixteenth birthday. It had begun to drizzle, and the car swerved out of control and crashed. Mandy's date was thrown clear of the convertible, un-injured. But Mandy died instantly.

Mandy's parents asked me to "give the sermon" at her funeral service because, they said, "Mandy talked about nothing more than Jesus, Luis Palau, and going to heaven."

On the day of the funeral, the church filled up with famous personalities, all of whom had a view of the casket that con-tained Mandy's body.

"Ladies and gentlemen," I said to these famous people, "what you see in the casket is not Mandy. It is Mandy's body, but the real Mandy is not here. Mandy is in heaven with Jesus Christ because the Bible says, 'away from these bodies . . . at home with the Lord' (2 Cor. 5:8). We're going to bury Mandy's body this afternoon. But the Bible says that the body is just the house of the soul and spirit—the essence of who we really are. Because Mandy had eternal life, she went straight to heaven when she died. Although her body will stay here, her soul and spirit went immediately to be with the Lord."

Mandy did not live a long time after she asked the Lord Jesus to be her Savior, but the years she had, she used well. She couldn't help but tell everybody she knew the exciting news about Jesus Christ.

That's genuine adventure, and it flourishes whenever and wherever enthusiastic followers of Jesus brag on their Savior.

Momentary vs. Lifelong

Excitement generally lasts only so long as high levels of endorphins and adrenaline course through the body. When they subside, so does the excitement—only a memory remains. Adventure has far more staying power. Because it blazes the trail of a bigger-than-life mission, it doesn't fizzle out after the fireworks die away. Adventure dances long after excitement goes to bed.

But you don't have to travel to Shanghai or Rome or to any other exotic city to find adventure. God has provided more than enough adventure for you right where you live—*if* you're willing to accept the mission he wants to give you. The Bible says he'd like to appoint you to a lifelong post in heaven's diplomatic corps. He offers you the impressive title of ambassador (2 Cor. 5:20), promises to provide you with all the resources you need to complete your assignment (Phil. 4:19), and gives you unlimited access to the Head of State for personal instructions, encouragement, or emergency insight (Phil. 4:6).

God loves to partner with his valued ambassadors to bring young men and women safely into his kingdom of love. When we're serious with God, the Lord always steps in—sometimes in amazing ways beyond anything we imagine.

One day two university students, both Christians, noticed two Chinese students who always seemed to stick together. The foreigners looked lonesome and appeared to speak only with each other. The two Christians befriended the Chinese students. Eventually they began to talk about Jesus Christ, and both of their Chinese friends became believers. Only later did it come out that these two students were the sons of a powerful government official in the People's Republic of China.

The next summer they announced, "We're going home for vacation instead of staying in the States. We want to share the Good News with our father and with the rest of the family."

How's that for unexpected adventure? The Americans didn't know of the connection between these two Chinese students and one of the most powerful men on Earth. They just served faithfully, and God used them.

When community or government leaders come to faith, a trickle-down effect often brings salvation to multitudes of regular citizens—especially in closed countries. I have no doubt that China's attitudes toward the West, toward freedom, and toward the church of Jesus Christ began to change because two young men at a university in the United States faithfully represented Jesus Christ.

But what if you've never met the children of powerful world leaders? What if you're "just" a high school student? It doesn't matter. If you accept the ambassadorship that God wants to give you, there's no telling what adventures await you.

Maybe you need to stop focusing on other people's flaws and take your own light of Christ out to the world. Begin to look outside the church walls for service and evangelism opportunities. If you accept the ambassadorship God wants to give you, who knows what the Lord could do with your life? These aren't just nice little feel-good stories. This is serious business for ordinary young men and women.

Bank on it: if you come to God on his terms, he will begin to open doors of adventure that you never envisioned.

Better Than Golf

Too many of us settle for excitement when we could grab adventure. We satisfy ourselves with a rush of adrenaline when what we really want is a lifetime of wonder.

I'm sixty-nine years old as I write this. I know many individuals my age who dream about spending their "golden years" playing golf, traveling from one course to the next, trying to outscore themselves and their buddies. Golf can be a great hobby, but is striving to know every blade of grass on every course on the face of the earth the *best* use of your life? You have many years ahead of you; why spend your days dreaming of hitting a little white ball when you can be winning souls for eternity? What really excites me is a lifetime of continued adventures in winning more men and women to Jesus Christ, knowing that their acceptance of Christ ensures their eternal happiness in heaven. That's real adventure. That's genuine excitement. And you can share fully in it the moment you take God up on his offer.

HOW TO FIND Adventure
ACCORDING TO THE BIBLE

1. **Choose the priceless over the expensive.**
   "Is anyone thirsty? Come and drink—even if you have no money! Come, take your choice of wine or milk—it's all free! Why spend your money on food that does not give you strength? Why pay for food that does you no good? Listen, and I will tell you where to get food that is good for the soul! Come to me with your ears wide open. Listen, for the life of your soul is at stake" (Isa. 55:1–3).

2. **Be certain you're chasing a worthy goal.**
   "We pleaded with you, encouraged you, and urged you to live your lives in a way that God would consider worthy" (1 Thess. 2:12).

3. **Maintain a sharp, single focus.**
   "I am focusing all my energies on this one thing: Forgetting the past and looking forward to what lies ahead, I strain to reach the end of the race and receive the prize for which God, through Christ Jesus, is calling us up to heaven" (Phil. 3:13–14).

4. **Be willing to forego earthly comforts.**
   "I once thought all these things were so very important, but now I consider them worthless because of what Christ has done. Yes, everything else is worthless when compared with the priceless gain of knowing Christ Jesus my Lord" (Phil. 3:7–8).

5. **Embrace a life of considered risk.**
   "But my life is worth nothing unless I use it for doing the work assigned me by the Lord Jesus—the work of telling others the Good News about God's wonderful kindness and love" (Acts 20:24).

6. **Make sure the rewards are worth your sacrifices.**

   "It was by faith that Moses, when he grew up, refused to be treated as the son of Pharaoh's daughter. He chose to share the oppression of God's people instead of enjoying the fleeting pleasures of sin. He thought it was better to suffer for the sake of the Messiah than to own the treasures of Egypt, for he was looking ahead to the great reward that God would give him" (Heb. 11:24–26).

7. **Admit your discomfort but keep in mind your future.**

   "For our present troubles are quite small and won't last very long. Yet they produce for us an immeasurably great glory that will last forever!" (2 Cor. 4:17).

8. **Keep fear under control.**

   "The LORD is my light and my salvation—so why should I be afraid? The LORD protects me from danger—so why should I tremble? When evil people come to destroy me, when my enemies and foes attack me, they will stumble and fall. Though a mighty army surrounds me, my heart will know no fear. Even if they attack me, I remain confident" (Ps. 27:1–3).

9. **Find a way to replenish your inner resources.**

   "We never give up. Though our bodies are dying, our spirits are being renewed every day" (2 Cor. 4:16).

10. **Remember that God loves to beat the odds.**

   "The best-equipped army cannot save a king, nor is great strength enough to save a warrior. Don't count on your warhorse to give you victory—for all its strength, it cannot save you. But the LORD watches over those who fear him, those who rely on his unfailing love. He rescues them from death and keeps them alive in times of famine" (Ps. 33:16–19).

WISE WORDS

LET THE BELOVED
OF THE LORD REST
SECURE IN HIM,
FOR HE SHIELDS HIM
ALL DAY LONG,
AND THE ONE
THE LORD LOVES
RESTS BETWEEN
HIS SHOULDERS.

Moses,
Deuteronomy 33:12 NIV

A Shield
All Day Long

All of us need to feel safe and secure. Yet few of us go to the extremes of Hamilcar Wilts, the unfortunate subject of an old children's story by Robert Yoder.[1]

"There never was a more careful man than Hamilcar Wilts," Yoder wrote. "Although the only river in his vicinity was two feet wide and looked badly in need of water, Hamilcar kept a rowboat on his roof in case of a flood. In the rowboat there was a raft, in case the boat leaked, and the raft's equipment included needles for sewing furs, in case Hamilcar was carried to the far north, and an auger for opening coconuts, in case he was carried to the tropics. There wasn't much against which Hamilcar wasn't prepared."

Hamilcar threw out all poisonous or combustible materials from his home and stocked his medicine cabinet with every potion known to man. He filled his home with fire extinguishers, lightning rods, and an elephant gun. Within his fortress, Hamilcar felt safe.

Eight miles away, however, lived a dolt named Boggle. Boggle blew up his house one day while trying to open a can of gasoline with a blowtorch. The explosion threw him seventy feet into a warehouse of pillows, where he landed gently. When Hamilcar heard the explosion, he thought something had damaged one of his trees, so he quickly donned a pair of lineman's gloves (in case of live wires) and a bee veil, hurried out to the yard . . . and promptly got crushed by Boggle's plummeting stove.

While few of us go to the lengths of Hamilcar Wilts, we all need to feel safe. We all look for security.

Bulletproof or Safe?

God built us with a need to feel safe and secure. When we don't feel safe, we look for all kinds of ways to find security, some of them extremely unhealthy. Sometimes we try to wall ourselves off from every possible threat. We don't allow anyone to get too close. We obsess over getting straight A's. We spend way too much time perfecting the "right" look. We want to feel bulletproof, invulnerable.

While tactics like these really can protect us from some dangers, they also make it impossible for us to enjoy real life. And in the end, they can't deliver real safety anyway (remember Hamilcar?). Real security is found not in a suit of armor but in a Guardian who faithfully surrounds us with his protection.

25 words or less The kind of bullets in an enemy's rifle don't matter. Whether they be lead or daisies, no projectile gets past God without his permission.

How is the safety we enjoy in God different from the bulletproof world that some try to create for themselves? And why does God's security program outperform anything else? Let me suggest five areas of superiority:

Bulletproof Life	Safety
• Flees from fear	• Frees from fear
• Avoids risk	• Embraces risk
• Falls back	• Forges ahead
• Closed outlook	• Open outlook
• Focused on danger	• Focused on opportunity

Superman may seem bulletproof—until someone starts shooting kryptonite bullets at him. But if God is his Guardian, then the kind of bullets in an enemy's rifle doesn't matter. Whether they be lead or daisies, no projectile gets past God without his permission.

Flees from Fear vs. Frees from Fear

No one wants to live in fear. We might go to the movies or rent a video to scare ourselves silly for a couple of hours, but nobody really wants to live out their days in the company of Dr. Hannibal Lecter.

Some folks so hate the feeling of fear that they'll do anything to keep it at bay. They wall themselves off, whether physically or emotionally. They run from any situation or opportunity that refuses to guarantee their safety. They try to avoid all dangers—but in fleeing fear, they become its prisoners.

True security comes not in fleeing fear but in facing it and tearing free of its iron grip. And how can we do that? The best way I know of is to place ourselves in the protective hands of God.

What promise from God makes you feel most protected?

The fact that every human being is going to die will always catch people's attention. I just praise God for his promise of eternal life when I die. I have accepted his Son, Jesus Christ, as my personal Savior, and that's as much protection as I need in this world and the next.

Bruce Crisman, BMX champion

As the psalmist prayed, "Keep me safe, O God, for I have come to you for refuge" (Ps. 16:1).

Before the Revolutionary War, an old British preacher named George Whitefield made several mission trips to the American colonies and frequently received death threats for his efforts. When friends would ask, "Aren't you afraid that you might be killed in America?" Whitefield would reply, "I am immortal 'til my hour has come."

That's true of every Christian. In fact, throughout my career I've banked on it. Many times during evangelistic campaigns, enemies of the gospel have threatened to kill me—often describing their plans in gruesome detail. I know I will continue to live until the moment God says, "Luis, come on up"—and then no one will be able to stop me from leaving. I am immortal until my hour has come. Scripture says it like this: "Every day of my life was recorded in your book. Every moment was laid out before a single day had passed" (Ps. 139:16).

Another encouraging Bible passage is Hebrews 13:5–6: "God has said, 'I will never fail you. I will never forsake you.' That is why we can say with confidence, 'The Lord is my helper, so I will not be afraid. What can mere mortals do to me?'" That was the passage my mother gave me when I left Argentina, and it has served me well.

A passage like this feels like a solid, massive rock under your feet. It tells you that God's unshakable presence will never leave you. He's with you on the front lines or in any other hot spot around the world. He's continually with all those who belong to Jesus Christ. Jesus said, "And be sure of this: I am with you always, even to the end of the age" (Matt. 28:20).

In this world filled with uncertainty and evil, you don't have to look far to find fear. And it does no good to try to wall yourself off from it.

Even when my sons were young, Colombia was a violent place—murder and mayhem everywhere. As the only blond-haired boys in the whole town of Cali, my sons stood out from the crowd. We had no guards, like the governor general did. When I traveled, Pat often stayed home alone with our sons. And I'd think, *Why am I doing this? Why bring children into the world and then leave them?*

One day some kidnappings took place not far from our neighborhood. I cried out to the Lord in despair, "I need a promise from you. I'm going back to the States. I can't just leave Pat alone without you giving me the assurance that you are going to protect her and the children."

And the Lord gave me Isaiah 54:13: "All your sons will be taught by the LORD, and great will be your children's peace" (NIV).

I underlined that verse in all my Bibles, both Spanish and English, and wrote the date: 1966. Andrew was born that February. It gave me tremendous peace to know that because our family had come to live in Colombia for God's purpose, he had promised, "I will take care of your sons. I will give them peace."

I know of no better way to find freedom from fear. I suppose we could have fled to a safer community, but God had called us for that period of our lives to Colombia. And no safer place exists than the spot to which God calls you.

Avoids Risk vs. Embraces Risk

In a frantic desire to shield themselves from pain, some people try to avoid all risk. They take off if they sense the slightest risk of failure. They imagine that by doing this they can avoid pain—but in fact, they end up missing most of life, the good along with the bad.

I'm a firm believer in risk. How can we accomplish anything worthwhile without risk? Since we don't know the future, we can't know for sure how this or that specific project might turn out—but that's half the fun! Many of the honored heroes of Scripture "risked their lives for the sake of our Lord Jesus Christ" (Acts 15:26; see also Rom. 16:3–4).

I learned a lot about risk from my mother, who started me out on the journey I've been enjoying now for more than forty years. Except for a risk she encouraged me to take, I might have settled for a comfortable career in international banking.

I was working as a teller at a branch of a foreign bank doing business in Argentina. One day a city official came to my line asking about getting funds to purchase six street sweepers from a company in America.

"I have to transfer the payment to Detroit," the official told me. "So what's it going to cost me in pesos?"

I told him I would check and return with the answer. I called headquarters in Buenos Aires. They kept me waiting, pretending to check on availability and exchange rates. In a few minutes the bank representative came back on the line and said, "It's thirty-eight pesos to the dollar, but let's say it's forty."

I told my manager, "Buenos Aires is selling us the transfer funds at forty pesos to the dollar, though it's really thirty-eight."

"Okay," he said, "tell the man it's forty-two."

In ten minutes we made 10 percent on the deal, plus charging a 3 percent service fee. But I felt we weren't telling the truth. *This is my city*, I thought. *They're really taking money from me, because I pay taxes.* The incident got my conscience going.

Soon afterward at a street meeting I preached from the Gospel of John. I felt the Lord saying to me, as clear as if he were sitting on my shoulder, "You hypocrite!" I had been telling the crowd, "If you receive the Holy Spirit, you will overcome temptation and speak the truth," knowing that tomorrow at the bank I'd lie to people over the counter.

So I talked to my mom. I was single and nearly twenty-five years old. My mom always wanted me to leave the bank for a ministry of preaching and teaching the Bible, but how could I?

For me safety in life comes from knowing all things work for good for those who love Christ. I love God's promise that no man can snatch me out of his hand. I think many people try to protect themselves financially. Overall America has created a look out for #1 mentality that contradicts teachings in the Gospels about not worrying about tomorrow.

Kyle Mitchell, Kutless

I had five sisters, one brother, and a widowed mother, and I was our family's primary support. That didn't matter to Mom. "Leave the bank," she said. "You can't go on like this."

Although the bank had given me a lot of freedom and a good salary, I approached the manager and said, "You know, I just can't do what we do over the counter. I feel that I'm lying." The man hardly flinched. Already they all called me "The Pastor," and he probably expected something like this.

"Well," he said, "you don't need to worry about it. You don't make those decisions; you just follow orders from headquarters. It's not your responsibility. You don't have to feel guilty."

Even as he spoke, I recalled the German soldiers in World War II saying the same thing: "I'm just following orders. I'm killing these people, but I'm just doing what I'm told."

I left the manager's office without saying any more. But the next day I still felt uneasy, so I told him, "I just can't do this."

"You know, you're on a track to become a manager," he replied. "You're going to go international—you'll be sent all over the world. And you're going to worry about *this*? Why jeopardize all of that?"

Because I hadn't planned what to say, I responded, "Well, if to become a manager I have to lie and cheat, I can't do it."

The guy hit the ceiling. I knew it was over. I'm amazed he didn't fire me on the spot.

A few days later an American walked up to my counter. We began talking, and I found out he worked with a Christian mission agency that planned to begin working in Argentina.

"If you know anybody who's bilingual," he said, "we're going to publish an evangelistic magazine, translating many of the articles from English. If you know of anybody, let me know."

"I'm your man," I said immediately.

So within four days of first speaking to the manager, I resigned from the bank. My mom celebrated my decision, even though I left for half the salary. Risky? Sure. But I had no regrets.

My family did go through some tough financial times after I left the bank. Nevertheless, my mom couldn't have been happier. Imagine if I had stayed in that institution, making money for overseas investors! I would have missed out on the privilege of helping men and women find an eternal home in heaven.

Falls Back vs. Forges Ahead

Defense might win championships in sports, but I doubt it's the best strategy for life. Constant worry about defending your territory, your resources, your heart, your schedule—it can't help but take a toll, and probably sooner rather than later.

Every day you see young men and women walking down school hallways or on the street who seem perfectly normal, in good health, well dressed . . . but in fact they are almost exploding with insecurities and fears. They can't move ahead in life because they're too busy retreating.

I know at least a little of what this is like, because as a young person I went through it.

For a year or so after I became a Christian, I felt really excited. Every Sunday I went to Bible class. But in an all-boys boarding school—especially a British-run boarding school, like where I went to school in Argentina—there tend to be a lot of boys with foul mouths who make fun of those who follow Jesus. Only about 3 of us in a school of 400 even went to Bible class, and there's nothing like 400 mean little British boys to make you feel like you're inferior. After a while I began to feel the pressure, and I began to cool down spiritually. I began to behave in many ways like I did before my conversion.

One day we were in an art class. The professor, Mr. Thompson, was an Englishman who smoked a pipe. Although the school was located in South America, it was like a little island of Great Britain. Mr. Thompson had just come from England, and we thought he didn't know a word of Spanish. So we always talked behind his back, saying nasty things about him.

How do you most often see people (or yourself) trying to protect themselves?

We play hide-and-don't-seek. "Ready or not, here I come" is our signal to find a safer place to hide. We avoid situations that might cost us something. More often, we hide our real feelings, opinions, and personalities, not wanting to expose ourselves to ridicule or criticism. We put on a happy face that tells others, "Don't seek my true feelings."

Rebekah Clark, editor

One day we were supposed to paint some trees, and I can't paint anything. Mr. Thompson looked at my painting and said, "Palau, that's terrible. Start trying harder." So when he was walking away, I said a dirty word about him in Spanish. And my classmates laughed. Mr. Thompson turned around, took the pipe out of his mouth, and demanded, "What did you say, Palau?"

But I wouldn't tell him. Now, the British run their boarding schools like the military. They have what they call a master on duty; he's like an army officer. My teacher said to me, "Go and see the master on duty." So I went.

Can you guess who was the master on duty that day? It was Mr. Cowan, a Christian professor who taught the Bible classes. I walked in and he said, "Why are you here, Palau?"

"Well," I said, head down, "I said a little something to Mr. Thompson."

"What did you say?"

I didn't want to tell him the dirty word I had used. He sat me down and said to me, "You know something, Palau? I've been watching you. Sure, you made a decision for Christ, and you come to the Bible classes in my home. But you know something? You are the biggest hypocrite in this school."

Wow! Out of 400 students, he says I'm the worst.

Then he did what the British always did when a student used foul words in school. He took a cricket bat—a flat, wooden paddle with hard rubber in the middle—and he gave me what they called "six of the best." I couldn't sit for three or four days.

But you know, far worse than the wallop with the cricket bat were his words, "You're the biggest hypocrite in this school." That really got to me—because it was true. I couldn't move ahead in my life because I was too busy retreating.

Closed Outlook vs. Open Outlook

There's no way to try to provide our own security without putting on blinders. We start to look inward, not outward, and we become cautious about everything. We don't notice the misery of others, nor do we care about their suffering, because we're too busy trying to safeguard our own little world. When we look to God to provide the security we need, however, our eyes remain free to start scanning the horizon for new opportunities.

After my dad died, our family quickly plunged from relative wealth to desperate poverty. We lost it all: property, farms, vehicles, servants. Everything disappeared, leaving us completely destitute.

Somehow we rented a house with one bedroom and a living room that we converted into a bedroom. We also turned the garage into a bedroom (that never could keep out the dust). At one point we owed eight months of back rent. Only the mercy of our landlord kept us from getting tossed onto the street.

Some days all we had to eat was a big loaf of French bread, flavored over the fire with garlic. On really good days we'd have one steak to divide among the eight of us. Yet at each meal we would get on our knees and pray to the Lord, thanking him for his provision.

You might think that such poverty would close my mom's heart, but it didn't. Her generous outlook prompted her to continue helping others. When a beggar came to the door, she gave what she could. She continued this pattern until the day she died. After we grew up, we learned there was no use in sending her money; she wouldn't buy herself anything. We gave her a piano once, and she turned around and gave it to my brother.

Mom lived out the message of Psalm 112:5–8:

All goes well for those who are generous,
who lend freely and conduct their business fairly.

Such people will not be overcome by evil circumstances.

Those who are righteous will be long remembered.

They do not fear bad news;
they confidently trust the LORD to care for them.

They are confident and fearless
and can face their foes triumphantly.

The whole time we lived in abject poverty, Mom gave us a strong sense of security. Through prayer and singing and by affirming the promises of God, she kept us from fear and despair. Mom challenged us to believe that God would provide in the nick of time. She continually quoted Bible promises to us, especially a few basic ones:

- "The LORD your God will go ahead of you. He will neither fail you nor forsake you" (Deut. 31:6).

- "So I tell you, don't worry about everyday life—whether you have enough food, drink, and clothes. Doesn't life consist of more than food and clothing? . . . Your heavenly Father already knows all your needs, and he will give you all you need from day to day if you live for him and make the Kingdom of God your primary concern" (Matt. 6:25, 32–33).

- "I am leaving you with a gift—peace of mind and heart. And the peace I give isn't like the peace the world gives. So don't be troubled or afraid" (John 14:27).

- "And we know that God causes everything to work together for the good of those who love God and are called according to his purpose for them" (Rom. 8:28).

- "And this same God who takes care of me will supply all your needs from his glorious riches, which have been given to us in Christ Jesus" (Phil. 4:19).

Mom recited these verses to us over and over during the toughest times. She'd tell us repeatedly, "God knows even the minute details of your life; they're all under his control." She encouraged us to expect God to provide—and he did, in unusual and unexpected ways. The truths she kept repeating became utterly real to us, and I fully believed them. I still do.

I'm absolutely convinced that genuine security comes down to knowing and believing the promises of God. So let me ask you: Are you confident that when the Lord makes a commitment, he never backs down?

What would happen, I wonder, if today we took the Word of God as seriously as we take the word of our doctor? We walk into his office, report to the front desk, and sit and wait. Eventually we get called to the examination room, where we wait some more. Finally the doctor comes in and prods and pokes and listens and looks. After a while he says, "I know what the problem is." He gets out a pad of paper, with a pen scratches a few illegible lines, and says, "Go to the pharmacist and have this prescription filled."

So we go to the pharmacist. Probably we have never met this person. But she gives us a bunch of red pills, yellow pills, and a bottle of green liquid. "When you get up in the morning," we hear, "take a spoon of this. And before every meal, take two of these pills." And we obey to the letter. We don't ask to see the pharmacist's license. We don't wonder if those pills contain chalk. We just get up in the morning and do what she said.

So why is it that when the Lord gives us a prescription or makes us a promise in his Word, we often say, "Now, wait a minute! We have to interpret this." If we treated the doctor and the pharmacist the way we treat the promises of God, we would end up dead.

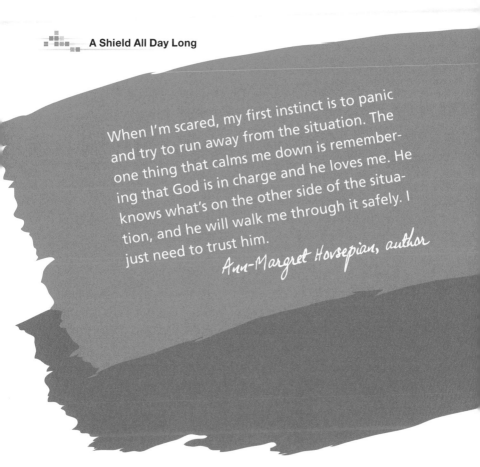

When I'm scared, my first instinct is to panic and try to run away from the situation. The one thing that calms me down is remembering that God is in charge and he loves me. He knows what's on the other side of the situation, and he will walk me through it safely. I just need to trust him.

Ann-Margret Hovsepian, author

The only true security lies in Jesus Christ. Only when we believe that he is everything, our all and in all, will we discover and enjoy genuine safety. Jesus is the Rock, our strong and permanent protector, and those who look to him for help radiate joy (Ps. 34:5). The Bible declares that all the promises of God are answered "yes" in Jesus Christ (2 Cor. 1:20)—in other words, they're all yours. And they're all true. So anchor your faith to the promises of God and enjoy true security!

Focused on Danger vs. Focused on Opportunity

Anyone who insists on trying to become emotionally or financially bulletproof can't help but ending up focusing on the dangers of life rather than its opportunities. And for that reason they usually end up with a pile of regrets.

When people look to find their safety in the power and love of Jesus Christ, they discover a new ability to focus on the opportunities ahead rather than the dangers. And so they avoid coming to the end of their life and saying, "I fear that my existence will have been insignificant."

My life was headed toward insignificance until I reached the age of seventeen. I refused to get serious about spiritual things. But that began to change as Carnival approached that year.

Carnival in Argentina happens forty days before Easter. Everybody holds big parties and goes dancing and drinking and gets into all kinds of stuff. Think Mardi Gras but with a Latin beat. After Carnival, everybody becomes "holy." But during Carnival, anything and everything goes.

Some friends of mine invited me to a wild party. But God was at work in my young, rebellious life.

The week of Carnival I found myself alone at my grandmother's house. And for the first time in almost four years, I started reading a Bible. I put it by my bedside and I prayed, "Lord, get me out of these dances. If you get me out of them, I'll serve you forever. If I go to these dances, I'll wreck my life. Who knows what I'll do, Lord. But I don't know how to say to my friends, 'I'm not going to go.' Do something, Lord. Get me out."

I wondered what God would do. I woke up the next morning, the first day of Carnival, and I felt something odd in my face. I had no pain, but when I looked in the mirror, I saw my face bloated like a fat balloon. It was almost like I had tennis balls inside my mouth. I don't know what happened, but I looked awful!

And I said to myself, "The Lord has answered my prayer."

How can a guy go to a dance looking like this? He can't. So I called up my friends. "I'm not going to the dance," I said.

"Why not?" they asked.

"I'm sick," I replied. "You should see my face."

They all came to the house, and when they saw me they said, "Oh, yeah—you can't come tonight." But Carnival is a week long. So they said, "Maybe you can come tomorrow or on the weekend."

But since I believed God had answered my prayer, I said, "Nope, that's it." Oh, I was still a coward; I didn't tell them why I wouldn't go. But when I walked back inside the house, I said, "Lord Jesus, I'm yours forever. I don't want to have anything to do with the world. I'm going to serve you."

I decided to move to another city where my mother had tried to start a new life. I started all over, as if I'd been converted for a second time. I began to study my Bible. I got involved in a local church. In a few months I began to speak to audiences of little children. The church used to hold evangelistic street meetings, and the elders let me say a few words, then a little more. And suddenly it was such fun to serve Jesus Christ. I had discovered that the only safety worth having is in Jesus Christ.

Nobody finds ultimate security by focusing on the possible dangers. They find it only when they focus on the opportunities God places before them. They choose the safety only Jesus can bring and enjoy a wild adventure in the bargain.

There's no reason you can't do the same thing.

Where Do You Find Security?

No one can make himself bulletproof, no matter how hard he tries. Living in this world means you get your share of pain, without exception.

Still, we all need to feel safe. Every one of us longs for a strong sense of security. How will we find it?

Some look for it in bank accounts, piles of possessions, and financial stability. Have you heard of the American businessman who thought he could provide security for a Mexican fisherman? As the American gazed over the ocean from a pier in a small coastal fishing village in Mexico, a tiny boat with a single fisherman pulled in and docked. The American saw several large yellowfin tuna on board and complimented the Mexican on the quality of his fish.

"How long did it take to catch them?" he asked.

"Only a little while," replied the fisherman.

"Then why didn't you stay out longer and catch more?" the American wondered.

"I have enough to support my family's immediate needs," replied the Mexican.

"What do you do with the rest of your time?" he asked.

"I sleep late, fish a little, play with my children, take a siesta with my wife, and stroll into the village each evening, where I sip wine and play guitar with my amigos. I have a full and busy life, señor."

"I am a Harvard MBA and could help you," the American insisted. "You should spend more time fishing and with the proceeds buy a bigger boat. With your earnings you could buy more boats, and eventually you could own a whole fleet. Instead of selling your catch to a middleman, you could sell directly to the processor, eventually opening your own cannery. You would control the product, the processing, and the distribution. Of course, you would need to move to Mexico City and then to America. From there you could run your growing business."

"But señor," the Mexican asked, "how long will this take?"

"Fifteen to twenty years," the businessman replied.

"But what then?"

"That's the best part," the American laughed. "When the time is right, you would sell your company stock to the public, becoming very rich. You wouldn't have to worry about anything. Your financial future would be secure."

"Then what?"

"Then you would retire to a small coastal fishing village, where you would sleep late, fish a little, play with your grand-kids, take a siesta with your wife, and stroll to the village in the evenings, where you could sip wine and play guitar with your amigos."

It doesn't make much sense, does it? Your entire life lies in front of you. Don't waste your time by trying to provide for yourself the security that only the Lord Jesus can deliver. Allow God to do what he does best: "Let the beloved of the LORD rest secure in him, for he shields him all day long, and the one the LORD loves rests between his shoulders" (Deut. 33:12 NIV).

HOW TO BE
safe
ACCORDING TO THE BIBLE

1. **Recognize that ultimate safety is available only in God.**

   "I will lie down in peace and sleep, for you alone, O LORD, will keep me safe" (Ps. 4:8).

2. **Whenever you feel threatened, run to God, not riches.**

   "The name of the LORD is a strong fortress; the godly run to him and are safe. The rich think of their wealth as an impregnable defense; they imagine it is a high wall of safety" (Prov. 18:10–11).

3. **Care more about God's opinion than people's opinions.**

   "Fearing people is a dangerous trap, but to trust the LORD means safety" (Prov. 29:25).

4. **Ask the Lord for safety.**

   "And there by the Ahava Canal, I gave orders for all of us to fast and humble ourselves before our God. We prayed that he would give us a safe journey and protect us, our children, and our goods as we traveled" (Ezra 8:21).

5. **Realize that habitual sin removes God's hand of protection.**

   "We know that those who have become part of God's family do not make a practice of sinning, for God's Son holds them securely, and the evil one cannot get his hands on them" (1 John 5:18).

6. **Understand that God himself placed you right where you are.**
   "LORD, you have assigned me my portion and my cup; you have made my lot secure" (Ps.16:5 NIV).

7. **Be generous with the resources God has given you.**
   "All goes well for those who are generous, who lend freely and conduct their business fairly. Such people will not be overcome by evil circumstances. Those who are righteous will be long remembered. They do not fear bad news; they confidently trust the LORD to care for them. They are confident and fearless and can face their foes triumphantly" (Ps. 112:5–8).

8. **Refuse to put your security in money or political leaders.**
   "Riches don't last forever, and the crown might not be secure for the next generation" (Prov. 27:24).

9. **When trouble does come, place your hope in the promises of God.**
   "For he will conceal me there when troubles come; he will hide me in his sanctuary. He will place me out of reach on a high rock" (Ps. 27:5).

10. **No matter what happens, take refuge in God.**
    "Keep me safe, O God, for I have come to you for refuge" (Ps. 16:1).

WISE WORDS

DEAR FRIENDS, LET US CONTINUE TO LOVE ONE ANOTHER, FOR LOVE COMES FROM GOD. ANYONE WHO LOVES IS BORN OF GOD AND KNOWS GOD. BUT ANYONE WHO DOES NOT LOVE DOES NOT KNOW GOD— FOR GOD IS LOVE.

the apostle john,
1 John 4:7-8

Finding
True
Love

Sex or
Love?

Josh McDowell often tells audiences of
college students, "Each one of you has
two fears. One is the fear that you will
never be loved. Second is the fear that you will
never be able to love someone else."

College students, of course, aren't the only ones haunted by
these twin fears. At times they chase us all. Maybe your own heart
feels the terror right now. Perhaps at this very moment you're one
of the millions of young people desperately searching for love. You
want it, you crave it, you need it—but somehow it continues to
escape you. Be honest—do you ever find yourself asking:

Will *I* ever be loved?
Will *I* ever be able to love someone else?

Driving from my old neighborhood in Portland, Oregon, I used to see an advertisement painted on a bus stop bench. "Call for love," it urged, followed by a phone number. "Only $3.75 a minute." Some people feel so desperate for love, they'll pony up $3.75 a minute to talk to a stranger.

The Bible gives you far better news than a 1-900 phone number. The Scripture declares that God created you for love. To love and be loved was God's original purpose for us all. When you and I give and receive love, every area of our lives becomes a marvelous experience. We enjoy the world in new, unexpected ways.

When we love and receive love in return, even the difficult roads of life grow smoother and less steep. When we come to understand what the Creator says about love, we discover for ourselves how to find it and enjoy it to the maximum.

The Gift of Sex

We all want to be loved. We long for someone to care for us from the heart, to treasure us and love our company.

But many of us struggle to find true love because we confuse it with something else. When a TV or movie hunk turns to his gorgeous girlfriend and says, with a leer and a nod to the bedroom, "Give me some love, baby," we all know they're about to have sex. Our culture has conditioned us to equate sex with love—but they're not the same thing at all.

The Bible teaches that God created human sexual impulses for our benefit. Our heavenly Father gives us all things to enjoy, including sex. Sex is not sinful or dirty, contrary to what some may think. It's clean and pure, wonderful and fun, even marvelous. And God reserved it for inside the bounds of marriage.

But what has happened? We have so corrupted the sexual relationship that many of us feel embarrassed even to talk about it. For many years during our campaigns and festivals, I've talked about God's view of sex. I usually get several letters of criticism. "You mustn't talk about those evil things," they scold.

Evil? Who said sex is evil? The Bible says sex is a gift of God. In the beginning he made man and woman and gave them the physical equipment necessary for enjoying one another sexually. Sex is not some nasty invention that happened accidentally along the way.

Think of sex like an automobile (and I'm not talking about the backseat). You can use it decently as a useful means of transportation, or you can use it to run over little old ladies. The problem is not with the car but with the operator.

In the same way, sex is great within the boundaries God set for it—but ignore those limits, and you become a danger to yourself and others. I enjoy reading, but I'd be a fool to devour a new book while driving in rush hour traffic. Likewise, in the Bible God sets an appropriate time and place for sex. Violate his directions, and you'll find yourself calling a tow truck very soon. Could that be why we see dented fenders, broken glass, and flashing yellow lights everywhere we go in America?

Adults like me in the church are partly to blame for this mess. We have not accurately taught what the Bible says about sex. My dad died when I was ten, and no one ever told me about the positive side of sex.

And what a positive side it is! The Scripture declares that a husband and wife become "one flesh" (Gen. 2:24; Matt. 19:5 NIV). The sexual relationship of a married couple, united in Jesus Christ, pictures something both marvelous and sacred: the unity of the soul with God. Sexual enjoyment in marriage is a gift of God to be enjoyed all through life. It's not love itself, but God invented it as a great way to express love.

The tremendous force we call sex is powerful—it can make you or break you. If you handle it right with the power of God, you can enjoy great success and feel happy and free. You will be able to look at yourself in the mir-

Sex is fun and enticing, but it can't substitute for love. Don't be content with less than what God wants to give you!

words or less

ror without shame or embarrassment. But sex can also destroy you—and one of the most common ways it does so is by masquerading as love.

Choose the Best

Because sexual activity binds people together in powerful and mysterious ways, God reserved it for a man and woman joined in marriage. Of course, sex can *feel* good even outside of those boundaries. But extramarital sex is something like drinking arsenic-laced Kool-Aid—sweet-tasting poison, deadly to the last drop.

Nevertheless, because we all want love—both to receive it and to give it—we grab any glimmer of love we can find. And let's be honest: love is a much rarer commodity than sex (even within marriage). Some of us have never experienced true love in our entire lives. So why not at least enjoy sex?

My answer: No one who wants true love has to settle for mere sex. Sex is fun and enticing, but it can't substitute for love. Why not go after the real thing?

Don't be content with less than what God wants to give you! True love, the kind Jesus Christ offers to help you find, surpasses the experience of sex in at least five ways:

Sex
- Goal is orgasm
- Values performance
- Emphasizes looks
- Desires to get
- Means to an end

Love
- Goal is intimacy
- Values person
- Emphasizes character
- Desires to give
- The end itself

Why settle for the sizzle without the steak when you can have both?

Goal Is Orgasm vs. Goal Is Intimacy

Those who want sex and those who seek love generally pursue different goals. While sex prizes orgasm, love craves intimacy. The first concentrates on the body, while the second focuses on the soul. The first desires to grow close physically and erotically; the second wants to draw near emotionally and spiritually. The trial of Rae Carruth, a former professional football player accused of murder, highlighted the distinction for me. Cherica Adams died from wounds suffered in a car shooting allegedly planned by Carruth. In the weeks leading up to the trial, the press consistently identified Adams as Carruth's "girlfriend," a description Carruth despised. "I didn't even know her full name," he insisted, maintaining she amounted to nothing more than a sex partner. Eventually a jury found Carruth guilty of conspiracy to commit murder, shooting into an occupied vehicle, and using an instrument to destroy an unborn child—his own (a son, born ten weeks prematurely because of the shooting).

Orgasm may be good, but it's a poor substitute for love.

Sex outside of marriage is ugly—it causes division, cruelty, perversion, guilt, and a tremendous sense of emptiness. I have never had sex outside of marriage, but I have spoken with hundreds who have, and almost to a person they describe an aching void inside. Illicit sex might feel exciting for a moment, but when it ends, many individuals hate and blame their "partner."

And some even pull a trigger.

There's a world of difference between developing an intimate relationship with someone you love and spending a hot session with an available body. Love "does not demand its own way," the apostle Paul says (1 Cor. 13:5). In fact, "it always protects" (1 Cor. 13:7 NIV). Protection like this can't be found in a condom but only within relationships where both individuals seek the other's best interests.

And how can you develop this kind of deep concern for someone else? The Bible says, "Try to live in peace with everyone,

Dude, check out a 65-year-old woman.
Probably not that fun to kiss
but she's someone's favorite grandma.
Physical attraction fades
but true love is enduring.

Kyle Mitchell, Kutless

and seek to live a clean and holy life, for those who are not holy will not see the Lord" (Heb. 12:14).

To be "holy" doesn't mean you become a phony, superficial, judgmental nut. Holy means you have nothing to cover up. Holy means you can look God in the face with a clear conscience and say, "Thank you, Lord, that I have nothing to be ashamed of, nothing to hide, no awful secret in some dark corner of my mind."

Did you know the Bible says your body is a sacred thing? "You yourselves are God's temple and God's Spirit lives in you" the apostle Paul said in 1 Corinthians 3:16 (NIV). Therefore we can't behave like cats, dogs, cows, or horses. That's why the Bible urges each of us to "honor God with your body" (1 Cor. 6:20).

God wants the best for us, and that means purity, happiness, and satisfaction. The Bible says, "God blesses those whose hearts are pure, for they will see God" (Matt. 5:8). Don't buy the lie of the media. It isn't great "fun" to have sex outside of marriage. Oh, I'm sure there's a certain thrill, but it goes away very fast, leaving behind guilt and emptiness and a deep sense of despair. Don't fall for it. The way of God is the best.

You may say, "Luis, I can't do it. I don't have the power." None of us has the power! But the Bible says, "When the Holy Spirit has come upon you, you will receive power" (Acts 1:8). God gives us the gift of sex to enjoy, and he gives us the power of the Holy Spirit to keep it under control. The Lord says to you, "I can keep you. I'll guard your heart. I'll protect you, I'll fulfill you, and I'll fill you with the Holy Spirit."

That doesn't mean, of course, that all your struggles immediately cease. Mine didn't! Many years ago a doctor asked a conference audience, "Have you ever thanked God for your body?" As I sat in the crowd I thought, *No, I haven't. All these temptations, all these thoughts cross my mind, and I know some aren't right.* I wondered what to do.

First, I discovered that while temptation comes to all of us, temptation isn't sin. Temptation is merely the desire to sin. But in the power of Jesus, you and I can overcome temptation. The Bible says, "I can do everything with the help of Christ who gives me the strength I need" (Phil. 4:13).

"But Luis," you reply, "I've already messed up."

I once spoke on this topic in Medellin, Colombia. After I finished, a charming sixteen-year-old girl ran up to the platform, weeping. "Mr. Palau," she cried, "does this mean there's no hope for me? Two years ago I had sex." She told me her father sexually abused her, and she felt so dirty that she turned promiscuous. "Can God ever forgive me?" she wanted to know. "Will God ever give me a decent husband?"

I told that brokenhearted young woman that God is good and compassionate. I assured her that the blood of Jesus Christ,

Our society is obsessed with the body—how it looks, how it performs, and how it feels. But the body is just a shell for the soul, which few people care about. No wonder they choose sex over love. They don't realize it's empty without the commitment of love (marriage). Love, on the other hand, is complete on its own.

Ann-Margret Hovsepian, author

which he shed on the cross when he died for our sins, would purify her conscience so she could serve the living and true God (Heb. 9:14). I admitted that some things might never be quite the same but insisted she could start over. If she came to God's Son and surrendered her past, her memories, her failures and immorality, Jesus would forgive her. And, I said, Jesus promised to make the power of the Holy Spirit available to her.

I'm telling you the same thing. Holiness *is* an option for you, no matter who you are or what you may have done. You too can join millions of others in choosing intimacy over mere sex.

I believe the best gift you can give your future marriage partner is purity—to be able to look deep into his or her eyes on your wedding day and have nothing to hide. Holiness means reserving something beautiful and precious to give one person when you say, "I do."

I have four sons, all married. It thrilled me to see each of my daughters-in-law walking up the aisle on her father's arm and to see each of my sons standing at the front, knees shaking! At each service I saw a pair of young people who love God, and who had remained pure by the power of God. I watched them get on their knees and look each other in the eyes with no secrets to keep hidden, no dirt, no guilt. They could gaze at each other on that happy day with bright smiles and say, "I belong to you and nobody else. I have nothing to cover up before the Lord."

I tell you, it's beautiful. And it can be yours.

Values Performance vs. Values Person

Walk into any bookstore and you'll have no trouble finding several shelves of books and manuals on sexual technique. Nearly all of them assume that if you become a more proficient lover, you will at last find the love you've always desired.

Sorry, but I don't think you will.

Better technique may increase sensual pleasure, but in place of genuine love, it may actually *increase* emotional distance.

Those who focus on performance rather than on the person inevitably devalue the sexual partner, who becomes little more than a handy receptacle for bodily fluids—and who dreams of becoming *that*?

Great lovers are not those who know how to push all the right erotic buttons but those who treat a loved one as an individual, not merely as a nicely assembled body. The main trouble with technique apart from love is that it almost always values conquests and trophies more than it does men and women made in God's image.

The story of Joseph in Genesis 39 illustrates my point. Joseph, a handsome and well-built teenager, worked for a wealthy Egyptian named Potiphar. Potiphar's wife made it clear (when her husband wasn't around) that she had noticed Joseph's attractive face and rippling muscles. "Sleep with me!" she told him. But Joseph refused. "How could I ever do such a wicked thing? It would be a great sin against God" he declared (v. 9).

Not easily discouraged, the woman kept approaching Joseph day after day with the same immoral proposition. She appeared so attracted to Joseph, so much in love. What a huge temptation! She had both riches and status—and who would find out?

One day while Joseph worked inside the otherwise unoccupied house, this lustful wife approached Joseph again with the same demand: "Sleep with me!" The godly young man once more refused, this time running out of the house.

No sooner had Joseph's feet flown out the front door than the woman turned against him. Five seconds earlier she supposedly loved him, but when he refused, she did a sudden about-face and tried to destroy him. She falsely accused Joseph of attempted rape and had him thrown in prison.

What a switch, from the desire for sex to the lust for punishment! What explains such a fast change? I think the answer is simple: wounded pride. The Bible says love "is not boastful or proud" (1 Cor. 13:4). The woman didn't love Joseph; she saw him merely as an attractive trophy. When it became clear she

What is one area in life where you see many people settling for "good enough" rather than pursuing God's best?

Definitely marriage. I think a lot of people marry because they feel pressured to get married instead of waiting for God's best and the unique man or woman God has for them. I feel that second to the decision to follow Jesus, marriage is the most important decision in life. A lot of people take it rather flippantly and I think that's partly why we are seeing so much divorce today. People are getting married for the wrong reasons, and instead of waiting for the one God has for them, they settle for what seems "good" rather than God's very best.

Another area in which I think people are settling for less than God's best is in their relationships with the opposite sex involving purity. Instead of approaching relationships as an opportunity to be godly and pure and to wait and let all your actions reflect purity, a lot of Christian young people are allowing impurity into their relationships. This is a subject I feel very passionate about, and I have been very vocal in encouraging single people in the area of sexual purity. It's something I am not just talking about, but I am really serious about living it in my own life.

Rebecca St. James

couldn't obtain that trophy, she set out to smash it. It's a pattern often repeated when sex-as-performance gets confused with love for the person. Why does this happen so often? Somehow, most people never stop to ask themselves a couple of important questions:

• Does anyone *really* find contentment by pairing up with dozens of sexual partners?

• Do such brief hookups *really* produce lasting happiness?

I'm not asking, "Does it feel good?" God created sex to provide intense sensations of physical pleasure, and that doesn't change just because the intercourse occurs outside of marriage. The Bible teaches that sin can indeed deliver pleasure—but only "for a short time" (Heb. 11:25 NIV). In the end, illicit pleasures always lead to enslavement and deception (Titus 3:3).

Remember this central truth: love is really about the person, not the performance. Love concerns much more than sexual technique and erotic novelty. It's about getting to know a person deeply, about caring for that person from the heart and developing a bond far stronger than anything that raging hormones can produce.

Emphasizes Looks vs. Emphasizes Character

When someone confuses sex with love, he or she usually emphasizes good looks over good character. I can't help but wonder if this confusion partially explains why so many Hollywood marriages go belly up.

One of the most publicized Hollywood breakups of the past few years was that of Tom Cruise and Nicole Kidman. It serves as a pattern for the rest. "Say it isn't so!" lamented one news flash. "Hollywood's golden couple are separating after 11 years of marriage."[1]

If nothing else, the breakup of Tom Cruise and Nicole Kidman demonstrated that great looks alone are not enough to keep a love affair going. Physical appearance can legitimately draw two people to one another, but it's never enough to keep them together.

We're all tempted to think that because we feel physically attracted to someone, we've found real love . . . but probably we haven't. Very likely it's just passion—very exciting, very real, but miles from real love.

Love involves body, soul, spirit, devotion, will, and emotions. Passion is purely sexual, often aroused by physical appearance. When someone says to a new boyfriend or girlfriend, "I love you so much I can't wait any longer to have sex with you," what they're really saying is, "I am sexually stirred by the way you look. My passion has been kindled, and I have to find physical release. I think you'll do."

"But Luis," you say, "I really *am* looking for love. I want to find someone. I want to have a boyfriend or girlfriend. I'm actively looking—and isn't sex part of it?"[2]

Believe me, if you want real love that will last forever, the physical side will come in due time. You don't have to jump the gun just because his or her looks drive you wild. The Old Testament hunk Samson chose looks over character, and his decision brought him no joy. When he saw a pretty face in a neighboring town, he told his parents, "Get her for me, for she looks good to me" (Judges 14:3 NASB). Over their objections, Samson married the girl. The marriage lasted only a few days and resulted in bitterness, hurt, and multiple deaths. In the end, Samson lost his wife and eventually his life.

So do looks mean nothing? I'd never say that. I think physical attraction should enter into the romantic mix, but it's not the only part and *certainly* isn't the most important part. Every study I know affirms that character counts for far more in a fulfilling relationship than does physical appearance. You can

Sex is temporary while love lasts even through difficult times. Love won't leave, it won't quit. Sex is selfish and only sticks around while it is convenient. Sex might satisfy a part of you, but love fulfills all of your needs. If you're just looking for sex, you'll get burned and used. If you look for love, you'll have more than just the physical benefits. You'll have someone who knows you, is committed to you, and wants what is best for you. You won't get that offer from anyone interested in a fling.

*Elizabeth Honeycutt,
contributing author,
Starting Point Study Bible*

hardly go wrong by focusing on character, but an unbalanced concern for looks often leads to heartache.

Too many magazines, books, television shows, and movies paint a totally unrealistic picture of sexuality. Our ministry counsels young men all over the world who have been deceived and enslaved by pornography. They have been gravely injured by a picture of sex that never has been and never will be true.

Be very careful about what you allow yourself to look at! If you toy with pornography, you contaminate your soul. You also run a high risk of addiction—and a downward spiral from there. You'll want more and more, but you will never find satisfaction. Jesus said, "I say, anyone who even looks at a woman with lust in his eye has already committed adultery with her in his heart" (Matt. 5:28).

On the other hand, the Bible gives the following counsel to young men looking for a godly partner: "Who can find a virtuous and capable wife? She is worth more than precious rubies" (Prov. 31:10). Looks count, but character counts for much more. And when we begin our search for character by tapping into the power of God, we can find a quality of life impossible to attain in any other way.

Best-selling author Zig Ziglar once told an audience: "On a very personal note, let me say I've always loved my family. . . . But I'm here to tell you that I had no idea what it meant to love until I learned to love through Jesus Christ. When you love your family, when you love your fellow human beings through Christ, there's a power and a love and a depth and a strength which is absolutely unimaginable to the nonbeliever."

He's right. The Bible says you can know *real* love, *pure* love, when you know God in your heart through Jesus Christ.

Desires to Get vs. Desires to Give

We've all met individuals who are far more interested in receiving than in giving. Most of us dislike spending much time with such self-centered people.

And yet a craving for sex apart from a commitment to love leads almost unavoidably to a nasty form of greedy self-love. Without love, sex becomes increasingly self-absorbed and selfish. Experiencing new pleasures becomes everything; the other person seems entirely irrelevant, other than his or her sexual equipment.

True love doesn't act that way at all. When you genuinely love another person, it thrills you to give him or her something precious. "It is more blessed to give than to receive" (Acts 20:35) is more than a biblical truth; it's a real-world fact. Nothing can compare to giving a special present to a loved one, especially a surprise gift. His or her joy cannot be bought at any price.

Giving lies at the heart of the Christian faith. The desire to give from a heart of love prompted Jesus to say, "Even I, the Son of Man, came here not to be served but to serve others, and to give my life as a ransom for many" (Mark 10:45).

Someday you'll probably be married, and the longing to give ought to characterize every Christian marriage. So the Bible says, "And you husbands must love your wives with the same love Christ showed the church. He gave up his life for her" (Eph. 5:25). The Scripture teaches that marriage partners should satisfy each other's sexual needs. They're to please one another, not deny each other (1 Cor. 7:5). In other words, it's mutual.

Sex within marriage in a solid Christian home gives genuine pleasure, joy, and satisfaction. Love wants the best for the other person and delights in giving. A man is most fully a man and a woman most fully a woman when they love each other with the sacrificial love of Jesus Christ.

But if you decide to reject the Bible's instruction on sex and love and instead choose to become a "bed buddy" with a boyfriend or girlfriend or just an available "someone," then you're headed for heartache. Recreational sex isn't at all like it's portrayed on television—fun, with unbelievably good physical sensations that leave both partners happy and without a twinge of regret or guilt. If you choose sex over love and decide to get rather than give, you'll much more likely wind up like a couple named Sarah and Andy than any of the beautiful, cool teenagers on *The OC*. Sarah's testimony reflects some of the heartache that wrong choices in the areas of sex and love can bring.

"If I had my time over again, I wouldn't have gotten pregnant and married so soon," she told me. "Not many of my

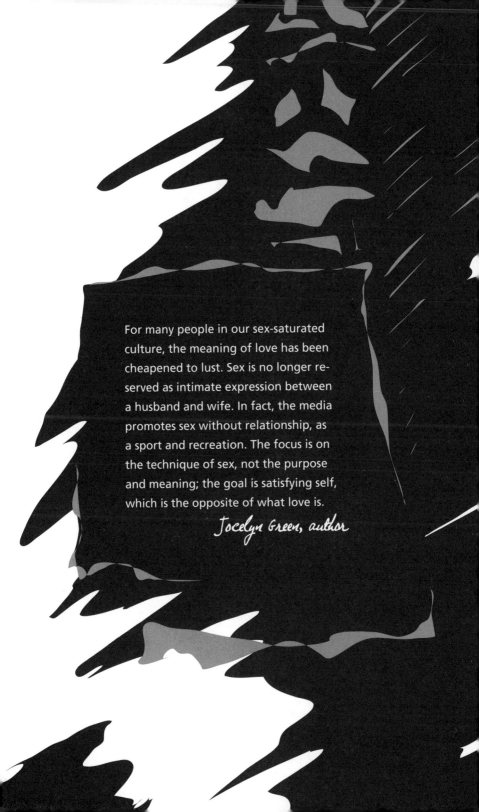

For many people in our sex-saturated culture, the meaning of love has been cheapened to lust. Sex is no longer reserved as intimate expression between a husband and wife. In fact, the media promotes sex without relationship, as a sport and recreation. The focus is on the technique of sex, not the purpose and meaning; the goal is satisfying self, which is the opposite of what love is.

Jocelyn Green, author

friends are married with babies already—and I feel jealous of them sometimes. One girl I know has a Porsche, and what have I got? A baby and this cramped little apartment and no money."

Hardly paradise. But Sarah and Andy wound up there when these two young people bought into the lies they saw so often on TV and in the movies.

"Andy and I met at school," Sarah continued, "and we got married when I was sixteen because I was pregnant. I'll never forget the panic. Andy was in the Army in Cyprus, and I was living at home with my dad, and I didn't dare tell him."

Again, hardly paradise. What little hope Sarah had, she thought she might lose. At the end of our conversation she told me, "I hope Andy and I will stay together, although being a soldier he's away a lot, and I get bored being stuck at home all day, so maybe one day we'll split up. The thing is, you have to try so hard to make marriage work, and divorce is so easy."

I have a friend who asked Christ into his heart very early in life. Despite living in a community where many if not most of his friends treated sex like a recreational pastime, he remained sexually pure (although not untempted!). He dated only other believers; he had little interest in dating someone who didn't share his spiritual interest. In fact, he said many times over the years, "I don't want to marry just a Christian; I want to marry somebody who loves the Lord. There's a difference." Just a few years ago he finally met the woman of his dreams, a beautiful young lady, and the two now have an effective ministry at their church. Is my friend sorry he waited so many long and sometimes frustrating years to go to bed with somebody? He has a one-word answer:

"HA!"

God doesn't reserve great blessings like this for a select few. They can happen in *your* life, too.

Means to an End vs. the End Itself

God designed sex as a means to express genuine love within marriage. He never intended sex to be an end in itself. When we treat food as an end in itself rather than as a means to sustain life, we become gluttons. When we treat a prescription drug as an end in itself rather than as a means to promote health, we become addicts. When we treat a job as an end in itself rather than as a means to provide the money we need to live, we become workaholics. In the same way, when we treat sex as an end in itself, rather than as a means to express love to a spouse, we open ourselves to a painful swarm of destructive behaviors.

Don't buy the lie of "recreational sex." Sex is far more than a form of fun physical exertion like a game of basketball or a leisurely bicycle ride. Sex is different because God *made* it different. Those who endorse "recreational sex" usually claim that it sets people free from restrictive, old-fashioned rules—but that's far from the truth. According to God's Word, "With lustful desire as their bait, they lure back into sin those who have just escaped from such wicked living. They promise freedom, but they themselves are slaves to sin and corruption. For you are a slave to whatever controls you" (2 Peter 2:18–19).

Sex outside of God's plan *always* results in slavery and emotional imprisonment, while when enjoyed within the Lord's boundaries it produces joy, peace, and freedom.

Jesus said, "So if the Son sets you free, you will indeed be free" (John 8:36). Free! Free to serve the Lord. Free to pray. Free to worship—and not with a guilty conscience or with a hypocritical smile. You live in freedom when you open your heart to Jesus Christ. The Bible says, "You will know the truth, and the truth will set you free" (John 8:32). Sexual satisfaction and freedom come when you know the truth that sets you free. Jesus Christ is *for* sexual satisfaction and freedom!

Someone may object, "But isn't God oppressive? Isn't he a joy-killer? He's always saying, 'Don't do this, don't do that.'"

No, just the opposite. Through the Bible, the Lord put up some fences and said, "Within this fence, you are free to do whatever you want. You can enjoy my gift. I installed the fences so you won't wreck your life. These are my rules to play and live by."

I believe many young people today are saying, "I want to know the rules." But you won't find them in magazine advice columns. You won't find them in a horoscope. You won't find them in most schools.

The only reliable place to find the rules is in the Bible. God created sexuality. The Designer who made us wrote the manual we call the Bible. If you live by the rules of God—not hiding behind masks, not putting on a facade, not settling for a show-business Christianity, but choosing the real thing—I tell you, you'll be a happy young man or a happy young woman. You'll be free! And you'll enjoy true love.

Love Makes the Difference

When the love of God invades a human heart, everything changes. Whites look whiter, reds look redder, blues look bluer. Love changes *everything*.

A friend of mine visited the Cook Islands in the South Pacific. On a boat trip around the turquoise-blue lagoon of Aitutake, a guide named Ke talked with a wide smile on his face and laughter in his voice. "Before the missionaries came, we were headhunters," Ke said. "You may have heard that these islands were named after Captain Cook, but that's not true. They got their name because we would cook you and eat you. But now we don't want to cook you; now we want to love you."

Love makes all the difference!

God made you to be loved and to love. But you can never experience real love, no matter who you are, unless you first know Jesus Christ. If you want genuine love, you must have the love of God in your heart—not just a few Bible verses tucked away in your brain, but God himself alive in your innermost soul.

And when that happens, you can experience for yourself what some anonymous writer has said so well: "Real love stories never have an ending."

HOW TO FIND Love
ACCORDING TO THE BIBLE

1. **Recognize that all true love comes from God.**

   "Dear friends, let us continue to love one another, for love comes from God. Anyone who loves is born of God and knows God. But anyone who does not love does not know God—for God is love" (1 John 4:7–8).

2. **Put your hope in God.**

   "Let your unfailing love surround us, LORD, for our hope is in you alone" (Ps. 33:22).

3. **Call out to God.**

   "O LORD, you are so good, so ready to forgive, so full of unfailing love for all who ask your aid" (Ps. 86:5).

4. **Love God's Son, Jesus Christ.**

   [Jesus said,] "Those who obey my commandments are the ones who love me. And because they love me, my Father will love them, and I will love them. And I will reveal myself to each one of them" (John 14:21).

5. **If you want to be loved, start by loving others.**

   "Those who refresh others will themselves be refreshed. . . . If you search for good, you will find favor" (Prov. 11:25, 27).

6. **Make specific plans to bless others.**
"If you plan good, you will be granted unfailing love and faithfulness" (Prov. 14:22).

7. **Don't look for sexual love outside of marriage.**
"The man who commits adultery is an utter fool, for he destroys his own soul" (Prov. 6:32).

8. **If you are married, look for ways to love your spouse.**
"A man is actually loving himself when he loves his wife" (Eph. 5:28).

9. **Don't harbor grudges, but be quick to forgive.**
"Disregarding another person's faults preserves love; telling about them separates close friends" (Prov. 17:9).

10. **Realize that love is more than an emotion; it must take action.**
"Dear children, let us stop just saying we love each other; let us really show it by our actions" (1 John 3:18).

WISE WORDS

THERE ARE
"FRIENDS"
WHO DESTROY
EACH OTHER,
BUT A REAL FRIEND
STICKS CLOSER
THAN A BROTHER.

King Solomon
of Israel,
Proverbs 18:24

A Friend Who Sticks Closer Than a Brother

Popularity or Genuine Connection?

A few years ago in Spokane, Washington, a group of college students looked at their empty bank accounts and decided they needed some money. After considering their options, they rented an empty storefront building downtown and put up a big, hand-written sign: "We listen, $15 an hour."

They gave no advice. Suggested no direction. Offered no prayer. They simply offered to listen for $15 an hour.

And people lined up by the hundreds to talk. The students made thousands of dollars just by listening.

You know the most surprising thing about this story? It could be repeated all over the world. Men and women so badly want human connection that they will share their most private thoughts with total strangers.

A cover story in *USA Today* headlined "Deep Secrets Told among Passengers on Airlines" reported how a thirty-one-year-old man suddenly started revealing his darkest secret to the stranger sitting next to him. The man confessed how his fiancée had spent the past year cheating on him and how he felt alone and betrayed. I trust the reporter's accuracy, because very similar things happen to me when I travel.

Why do people seek out a heart-to-heart talk with a stranger? According to *USA Today*, they do it because it feels safe. Second, strangers don't pass judgment like family members often do. Third, strangers don't tattle, because they don't know the individual who's "confessing." All three factors create what psychiatrists call "instant intimacy."

Instant intimacy has a big problem, however: it's more instant than intimate. We pour out our hearts to strangers because we don't have close, trusted friends to whom we can safely reveal the secret fears and hidden longings we keep locked away.

God built us for friendships, for rich, fun connections with others. Our hearts long for the kind of spiritual friendships that don't get hurt by miles of distance or years apart. After big victories or terrible defeats, we long to get on the phone with a friend whom we know will genuinely care. When we need a concerned ear, we spend whatever it takes to get in touch with a trusted friend.

So long as we have one.

Popular but Lonely

While all of us recognize the need for trusted friends, we're not at all sure how to find and develop them. In a continual crunch for time, we open wide our net and try to make as many positive acquaintances as possible. Soon we mistake popularity for genuine connection—and then we can't figure out why we still feel so lonely.

Things won't change until we recognize the huge gap between popularity and a genuine connection with other human beings. Popularity may offer a boatload of superficial, shallow acquaintances, but true friendship provides deep heart-to-heart connections that can mature into relationships that give life.

Opting for the Best

It's no sin to be popular, of course. Everyone wants to be liked. If God frowned on the idea of popularity, then what would we have to say about Jesus? As a young boy, "he was loved by God and by all who knew him" (Luke 2:52). At the beginning of Jesus's earthly ministry, everyone "spoke well of him" (Luke 4:22). And just days before Jesus's crucifixion, his enemies saw the crowds all around him and exclaimed, "Look, the whole world has gone after him!" (John 12:19).

The danger isn't in popularity itself but in mistaking popularity for friendship. And by chasing popularity in place of genuine connection, we only make the error worse.

While friendship may be harder to develop than mere popularity, it also has a much bigger payoff. Let's look at five ways in which genuine connection blows popularity out of the water.

Popularity	Genuine Connection
• Gives ego boost	• Provides reservoir of strength
• Flavor of the day	• Lasting favorite
• Craves compliments	• Seeks truth
• Known widely	• Known deeply
• Seeks to be a star	• Desires to be a friend

 words or less All of us, whether we're "popular" or not, are made to build real and deep connections with others.

All of us, whether we're popular or not, are made to build real and deep connections with others.

Gives Ego Boost vs. Provides Reservoir of Strength

No doubt about it: Popularity makes a person feel good. We might feel a certain kick in playing the role of the outsider or the lonely bad boy, but if given the choice, most of us would choose popularity in a heartbeat.

But ego boosts, no matter how frequent or big, don't have enough power to keep us going when real trouble hits. You need a true friend, not an autograph hound, when life turns hard. A genuine and deep connection to another human being provides a reservoir of strength that popularity just cannot match.

Every Wednesday when I'm home, I get together at 6:30 in the morning with a group of nine business and civic leaders from our community. We meet to pray and to encourage one another. Most of these men have become close personal friends.

A few years back our group began to pray for a man who then served in the U.S. Senate. In a letter we told him we were praying for him. Terrible family problems hounded this man, and eventually he felt as though everyone had abandoned him. On a visit to our area he asked us, "May I visit your prayer meeting?" For most of his political career he had enjoyed tremendous popularity. But because he never spent the time to forge deep, lasting connections with caring individuals, he found himself with nowhere to go when his world caved in.

Wherever you look in America, people feel lonely. Some pay enormous amounts of money to feel less alone. Others without great financial resources feel confused about where to turn. Because the Lord knew this, he created his own club, his own society, to address the need. He calls it the church, the body of Christ, the family of God. It is there that God encourages us to connect at a deep level with others in his family.

I am who and what I am today largely because of a loving church that took me in, encouraged me, and taught me the Bible when I first showed up on the church doorstep a few months before my eighteenth birthday. It was okay that I didn't do everything perfectly. They were with me for the long haul. They were choosing to invest themselves in me. Without them, who knows where I might have ended up?

Friends provide a reservoir of strength in challenging times. Popularity? It doesn't offer even a shot glass of lukewarm water.

Flavor of the Day vs. Lasting Favorite

Popularity comes and goes, depending upon the day and the current fashion. You can be popular one minute and forgotten the next.

Off the top of your head, can you name the members of the rock group Pearl Jam, the most valuable player of the 1998 World Series, or the 1996 presidential and vice presidential nominees of the Republican Party? No? Well, at one time, they all enjoyed tremendous popularity. These days you need a good encyclopedia or Internet connection even to find out their names.

Close personal connections, however, survive the passage of time. We'll always hunger for good, long-term friends.

Pat and I treasure our longtime friendship with a couple from Bellingham, Washington. They're not popular speakers; they're not rich. They're just "ordinary folks." But Pat and I seldom feel more comfortable than when we spend time in their home. We've known them for almost forty years, and we feel comfortable with them, accepted, completely at home.

How many friends do *you* have, I wonder, with whom you can feel comfortable and relaxed, at ease and happy, with no need for putting on a show or pretending to be something you're

How do you keep popularity from being your goal when your career depends on having fans who love you?

If popularity were my only goal, the hardships of touring would not be worth it. The life of a touring musician is not as glamorous as people think, and I'm often reminded that only Christ can be the motivation for what I do.

Kyle Mitchell, Kutless

not? No masks, no games, no pressure—just the satisfied feeling of being yourself and "at home."

One word of caution, though: Long-term friendship doesn't mean nonstop contact. You can connect with people without hanging out on their doorstep day and night. We need to set clear boundaries and establish appropriate fences. Proverbs 25:17 says, "Don't visit your neighbors too often, or you will wear out your welcome." We need boundaries to create healthy relationships—and that, of course, includes healthy boundaries between boyfriends and girlfriends, and even among "just friends" of the opposite sex. Sexual temptation often hits those who open up too much. If you get too close to each other, it's easy to slide into dangerous areas when you run out of things to talk about. Set boundaries around your conversation and how often you get together. Then don't cross those boundaries—you can't afford the risk.

Craves Compliments vs. Seeks Truth

Most individuals believe that to remain popular they have to hide their "ugly side." They worry that if the truth were ever discovered, their popularity would vaporize (and most of the time, they're right). So they create and try to live in a fantasy world of airbrushed facts, sugar-sweet flattery, and ego-inflating compliments.

While true friends speak with kindness to one another, they don't hide the truth. Avoiding unpleasant facts may help to keep someone popular, but in the end it acts like a cancer on true friendship. "Wounds from a friend are better than many kisses from an enemy," says Proverbs 27:6.

The truth can frighten us, however, and I suspect that's one reason some of us collect a lot of acquaintances but few close friends. We refuse to take the risks required by honest friendship.

And there are risks. What if your honesty angers your friend and he slams the door in your face? What if the truth forces your friend to make unwanted changes? What if you're wrong in your perception of "the facts"? What if you tell a friend the truth, thinking she'll feel grateful, but instead she attacks you for sticking your nose in where it doesn't belong?

Honesty with a friend can really be risky—but without it, you can never develop personal connections capable of giving you strength in the tough times and delighting you in the good ones. Friendships based on truth grow stronger when trouble hits, but acquaintances who know only how to flatter others stick around only while the fun lasts.

True friendship gets its toughest test after failure. That's when you discover your real friends. Genuine friends will tell you to your face that you messed up, then put their arm around you and figure out how, together, you can recover. Fans just walk away and look for new celebrities to worship.

Let's face it: friends make mistakes. More than once close friends of mine have made terrible mistakes in interpreting my words or actions. They made me angry, but I knew that they loved me. I knew their words came from pure love and nothing else. Friends don't always see or say things right, but you don't get rid of them because they ticked you off.

Some time ago Pat and I stayed for a few days with some friends. At one point our hosts had a loud and angry fight. The wife disappeared into the couple's bedroom for a long and tense four hours.

In her uncomfortable absence, I got alone with my friend in the living room and tried to get him to talk. I made some simple comments about husband-wife relationships, about how we all go through cycles when we can't explain why we lose self-control. Suddenly this proud man who doesn't like to show weakness began to pour out his story.

Honesty involves risk, and not everyone responds to the truth in the same way. Sometimes a person opens up, you offer help, and the friendship dies. Friendships can disintegrate; that's part of the risk. But why would anyone choose the alternative? No one wants to feel lonely and alone.

During a midnight television broadcast of *Night Talk with Luis Palau*, a young boy called our program. "Mr. Palau," he said, "I'm all alone, and it's so scary out here."

"Why are you alone?" I asked.

"My dad is gone somewhere, in a bar."

"And where's your mom?"

"She left us four years ago, when I was eight."

"What time will your dad come back?"

Being single in your early thirties doesn't carry the stigma it did a generation ago, but there can still be that sense that something is missing. Wallowing in self-pity, however, only increases any feelings of loneliness. To combat that, I seek opportunities to reach out to others with the gifts God's given me. It's amazing how connected you can feel!

Ann-Margret Hovsepian, author

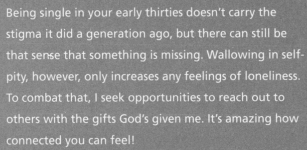

"Probably four in the morning. And I'm so lonely and so scared."

"Tomorrow night you come to the crusade at the stadium," I told him. "I'm going to introduce you to a bunch of people who are going to love you."

When the boy showed up the next day, I gave him a big hug and we prayed together. What a lovable kid! And so lonely. This twelve-year-old gave his life to Jesus Christ, and we introduced him to a local youth group. The church took the boy under its wing and cared for him. Today he no longer feels so lonely.

A word of caution here. Don't expect from friendship more than friendship can deliver. If you're looking to a human friend for what only God can supply, you're going to be disappointed. Don't demand from your friend what only Jesus Christ can give you.

A merely human friend can't give you fulfillment, peace, or joy, but Jesus specializes in all three. He obtained them for you on the cross, explaining before his death, "the greatest love is shown when people lay down their lives for their friends" (John 15:13). And he says to us, as he did to his disciples, "I no longer call you servants, because a master doesn't confide in his servants. Now you are my friends, since I have told you everything the Father told me" (John 15:15).

"Friends." Coming from Jesus, it has a nice ring, doesn't it?

Known Widely vs. Known Deeply

If one intimate friend is good, would twenty be better? Thirty? Fifty? A thousand?

Not necessarily. I don't believe you can develop a lot of close friends. Popularity may scream for crowds of adoring fans, but genuine connection cannot happen with no limit. While popularity leans toward width, friendship thrives on depth.

Why the difference? Those who want to be popular don't need to spend time with their admirers; their interests lie in receiving, not giving. The greater the number of fans, the better—and it doesn't matter much whether they're near or far away. So long as you can hear their applause, they serve their purpose.

Close friends, however, have to be developed. You can't expect an intimate friendship without spending significant amounts of time with your friend, one-to-one.

Experience tells me that each of us has different capacities for maintaining close friendships. Three or four is more than enough for some. The way their life boxes them in, the way their responsibilities demand their attention, they can't handle more—and they shouldn't feel guilty about it.

Really, you don't need dozens of friends. You can befriend only so many people. Time doesn't allow for more. Even Jesus developed only a few close friends during his earthly ministry. You could think of his "friendship life" as a series of circles.

In the outer ring stood the crowds who surrounded him wherever he went. Jesus ministered to them and taught them and loved them, but he didn't choose them for his closest friends. In the next circle we see a smaller group of devoted followers, numbering anywhere from 72 (Luke 10:1) to 120 (Acts 1:15). The men and women in this group ministered with Jesus and represented him to others, but they couldn't necessarily be called close friends. Step another circle closer to the center, and you find the Lord's core group of twelve disciples. He ate with these men, traveled with them, challenged them, led them. He called them all his friends, even though one betrayed him.

Still, these men didn't qualify as his closest friends. That privilege went to three disciples in the circle, just one ring from the center. Peter, James, and John knew Jesus better than anyone on Earth. It was these three whose help in prayer he requested just before his arrest and crucifixion (Matt. 26:36–46).

But at the very center of all these circles stood one man, John, whom the Bible consistently calls "the one Jesus loved"

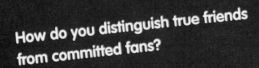

How do you distinguish true friends from committed fans?

True friends will talk about Kutless last rather than first. My true friends care more about how I'm doing as a person and how my individual walk with Christ is doing.

Kyle Mitchell, Kutless

(John 13:23; 21:7, 20). We have to consider John the Savior's closest earthly friend.

The example of Jesus suggests that if you value close friendships over popularity, you can't have a lot of intimate friends. Life simply doesn't allow for it. Instead, resolve now to develop a few rich, heart-to-heart connections.

So where can you find your closest friends? First, look for someone whose heart beats with yours on the most important issues. For a close friendship to develop, you must have something important in common, similar dreams, goals, and views of life. Think of close friendship as a form of teamwork. "If one person falls, the other can reach out and help," says Ecclesiastes 4:10. "But people who are alone when they fall are in real trouble." The book of Proverbs adds, "There are 'friends' who destroy each other, but a real friend sticks closer than a brother" (18:24). We all need a few friendships like that. And how do we grow and strengthen them once we've made the connection? You have to spend a lot of time talking about the deep and serious things of life. Intimacy cannot develop without opening up to each other and exposing your heart.

I considered the late Ray Stedman as one of my most intimate friends. Though two years could go by without us seeing each other, if I picked up the phone or he called me, it was as if we had spoken to each other the day before.

How did we get to that point? Mainly through his selfless love. From the moment he met me during a missions trip to South America, he took the initiative to grow our friendship. I knew he would stand with me if I had done the worst thing in the world. He never walked out on me, never gave up on me, but made it a habit to go out of his way to help and encourage me.

Who is *your* "Ray Stedman"? Who can you count on to give you the help and encouragement you need, no matter the circumstances? Maybe you don't have such a friend right now—but wouldn't you like to have one? If so, start doing the things today that allow you to build strong friendships that last and bring you joy.

Seeks to Be a Star vs. Desires to Be a Friend

Judy Garland was perhaps the greatest entertainer of the twentieth century. With a gorgeous voice and powerful screen presence, the woman who portrayed Dorothy in the film classic *The Wizard of Oz* commanded worldwide attention. Yet toward the end of her life she told a writer for *Forbes* magazine, "If I'm such a legend, why am I so lonely?"

A legend? You bet. Famous? All over the world. Popular? No question. Yet Judy Garland died in the middle of the night from an accidental overdose of drugs—a broken and lonely woman.

Unfortunately, the same kind of thing continues to happen today. Robbie Williams, a thirty-year-old pop megastar in his native England, recently told a London newspaper that he feels so lonely and unhappy that he has felt tempted to go back on the booze, for which he was hospitalized a few years ago.

Philip Hodson, a fellow of British Association for Counselling and Psychotherapy, told the paper: "I have treated many people who appear to have it all but suffer from depression. We call this Paradise Syndrome and it's common among celebrities and very successful people. Despite the glitz and glamour their huge wealth brings them, they just don't know what direction their life is going in."[1]

Stardom may shine brightly for a while, but it gives out an erratic light that feels icy cold. Genuine connection may not attract the glare of the media, but the arms of a genuine friend provide a comforting and steady warmth.

Which do you choose?

If you choose friendship, realize that you're going to need help in developing the solid connections with others that you really want. If you genuinely desire to get close to others at the deepest level, you can't do it alone. The media can't help you; money can't help you; not even Dr. Phil can help you. The deepest form of friendship forms only with divine help.

When Jesus lives in your heart, other friendships become more meaningful, more valuable, more fulfilling. Why? Because you feel at peace. You don't depend upon some flawed human to become your closest friend.

I personally live by this philosophy. Without question, Jesus Christ is my best friend. If everyone else let me down, I'd feel horribly disappointed and sad, but I wouldn't get desperate. I know I have a friend who will never leave me and never forsake me. I know I can depend on him completely.

Did you see Tom Hanks in the movie *Castaway*? His portrayal of a man stranded alone on a tiny South Pacific island earned him an Academy Award nomination. Hanks's character couldn't stand the isolation, so when a volleyball washed up on shore, he used his own blood to paint a face on it, gave it hair of weeds, named his creation "Wilson," and made it his best friend. He spoke to it, yelled at it, stroked it, embraced it, and almost lost his life for it when it drifted away on strong ocean currents.

Hanks unforgettably illustrates the human need for friends. But he also makes me wonder: Would I need a Wilson if I were marooned in the middle of the wide, blue ocean? Honestly, I don't think so. I'd feel achingly alone, sure, and I'd try my best to get home. But I don't think I'd need a Wilson; I already have a best friend named Jesus. And I'd much rather talk to him than to a volleyball with bad hair and a bloody nose.

Settle your friendship with Jesus Christ, once and for all, because only he can give you inner peace, real rest, and a sense of balance.

Friendship Basics

What should you do if you really want to develop a few close friendships but you're not sure how to start? What should you keep in mind? Allow me to suggest a few guidelines in your efforts to get connected.

Be a friend to win a friend. Proverbs 18:24 suggests that anyone who wants friends must first be a friend. People will then feel drawn to you. At the same time, realize that friends don't just show up on your doorstep. In rare cases friendship begins instantly, but then it takes genuine give and take. It isn't a one-way street. You must work at friendship; it doesn't grow automatically.

Don't try to push friendship. You can't demand friendship or manufacture it. You can water it, develop it, and strengthen it, but it happens one step at a time.

I just "bumped into" most of those who became my friends, and our relationship developed from there. I remember a businessman who tried to force a close friendship between us, but the nature of his personality made it impossible. Nothing ever happened.

Don't expect instant connections. Even after spending four years with a high school buddy, you may not know much about the person. So see how the friendship goes. Observe how he or she responds in a variety of situations. Then ask yourself, "Is this going to be worth pursuing? Is this going to be a lifelong connection or just a passing thing—good but temporary?"

Make sure you're trustworthy. Friendship demands trust. Can your friends trust you? If someone tells you a secret, does the information stay just between you two? If you make a promise, do you keep it? If you say you're coming at 8:15, do you come at 8:15? Don't expect that real friends will bear with your untrustworthiness. That's a friendship killer.

Look to give more than you get. You don't make friends in order to get something. If you try it, you're bound to fail. Many individuals don't have friends because they want only to receive, not to give. They feel a void in their inner person and want someone else to fill it. True friendship is a give and take. Make up your mind to give more than you take.

Recognize that healthy friendships lift you up. A healthy friendship lifts you up; a sick friendship drags you down. While you look to encourage and raise up the person you befriend, also make sure you pick friends who encourage you and make you into a better person.

Make sure you have realistic expectations. Answer the question, "What am I looking for in this friendship and why?" Above all, realize that your friend can't give you everything you need. Never expect a friend to supply what only Jesus Christ can deliver.

Identify potential friends within your normal range of activity. Make a list of the people with whom you believe you could develop close friendships. Begin to show respect and love for them. Friendship happens where you live, go to church, and go to school. Look around and ask, "Who are the kind of people to whom I'd like to feel close? In what areas could we help each other?" Certainly you can't go shopping for friends like you're looking for fresh vegetables at the supermarket—but you can keep your eyes open.

Look for young men and women with big vision. It's fun to have friends with huge dreams. I enjoy friends who want their lives to make a difference in the world. I also enjoy people who don't always insist only on having fun. My kind of friends enjoy the moment, the nice things of life, a good party, but they also concentrate on how to do the most good in the least amount of time.

Look for spiritually serious friends. Someone with a reputation as "the life of the party" may be a lot of fun during the good times but lifeless and a real drain otherwise. Those who take their commitment to Jesus Christ seriously but who can poke fun at themselves provide your best bets for potential friends.

Don't test your friendship. A friendship either exists or it doesn't. You don't need to spend your life trying to figure out if someone is really your friend. You're either a friend and you know it, or you aren't. Never try pushing the boundaries in order to test the strength of your friendship, to see whether your friend will stick by you. That's a test you can fail just by handing it out.

Pray. Ask God to open your eyes to the friends he might have for you.

The Cure for Spiritual Loneliness

God created us to live among friends. All of us long for the sort of companion the Bible speaks about, a friend who sticks closer than a brother (Prov. 18:24). I believe that friend is Jesus Christ. He is the only one who can fill the profound vacuum at the level of spiritual loneliness.

During a campaign in Tyler, Texas, I received a call one night from a deeply discouraged fifteen-year-old young man. Brent told me that he "used to be into God a lot, and go to church, but I don't believe in God anymore." It turned out his parents were divorced, his grandfather had cancer, he had been "busted for marijuana and stuff like that," and life just didn't seem worth living anymore.

He told me that both his parents were looking for a way to send him away "because they don't want to keep me." He insisted his mother was "crazy" and revealed that his dad "goes to the club every single night, night after night, and he leaves me here all by myself. And because I'm on probation I can't leave. So I'm here and I can't talk to anybody. I'm just here all by myself and I sit in the dark and I wonder, *why did God put me here?*" As much as it tore me up to hear it, it didn't particularly surprise me to hear Brent say that he had considered committing suicide.

I told Brent that he had every right to feel angry that his parents didn't give him the kind of love and care that he needed, but that God wanted to be his Father. I told him that God had promised to never leave him or forsake him, and I quoted a wonderful Bible promise to him: "Even if my father and mother abandon me, the Lord will hold me close" (Ps. 27:10). I also told him that I would put him in touch with people who would love to welcome him into their church and give him a new family among mature Christian believers. And I told him that I believed God wanted to use him to help other struggling teens.

That night, it was my privilege to lead Brent to a new life in Christ. He accepted Jesus as his Savior, and we put him in touch with a solid church in his area, full of mature believers delighted to open their arms to him.

You see, loneliness can be cured! Jesus Christ died and rose again so that we might call him "friend" and so that we might be linked together as brothers and sisters in God's family. Everyone has moments of being alone, but we never have to feel isolated and lonely again.

Jesus makes sure of that.

HOW TO GET Connected
ACCORDING TO THE BIBLE

1. **Admit your need for others.**

   "If one person falls, the other can reach out and help. But people who are alone when they fall are in real trouble. And on a cold night, two under the same blanket can gain warmth from each other. But how can one be warm alone? A person standing alone can be attacked and defeated, but two can stand back-to-back and conquer. Three are even better, for a triple-braided cord is not easily broken" (Eccles. 4:10–12).

2. **Develop a few close friends rather than a boatload of acquaintances.**

   "There are 'friends' who destroy each other, but a real friend sticks closer than a brother" (Prov. 18:24).

3. **Be gently honest with others, and genuinely value their honesty in return.**

   "Wounds from a friend are better than many kisses from an enemy" (Prov. 27:6).

4. **Recognize that true friendship will require self-sacrifice.**

   "Follow God's example in everything you do, because you are his dear children. Live a life filled with love for others, following the example of Christ, who loved you and gave himself as a sacrifice to take away your sins" (Eph. 5:1–2).

5. **Remember that no one likes to hear you talk incessantly about yourself.**

   "Do not be conceited" (Rom. 12:16 NIV).

6. **Be more concerned about who a person really is than his or her social status.**
   "Do not be proud, but be willing to associate with people of low position" (Rom. 12:16 NIV).

7. **Throttle your selfish instincts and look for ways to show respect to others.**
   "Take delight in honoring each other" (Rom. 12:10).

8. **Refuse to give bitterness any place in your soul.**
   "Be kind to each other, tenderhearted, forgiving one another, just as God through Christ has forgiven you" (Eph. 4:32).

9. **Don't concentrate merely on your own fun, but think of ways to reach out to others.**
   "Think of ways to encourage one another to outbursts of love and good deeds" (Heb. 10:24).

10. **Find a good church and build God-centered friendships there.**
    "And let us not neglect our meeting together, as some people do, but encourage and warn each other, especially now that the day of his coming back again is drawing near" (Heb. 10:25).

WISE WORDS

COMMIT YOUR WORK TO THE LORD, AND THEN YOUR PLANS WILL SUCCEED.

King Solomon of Israel, Proverbs 16:3

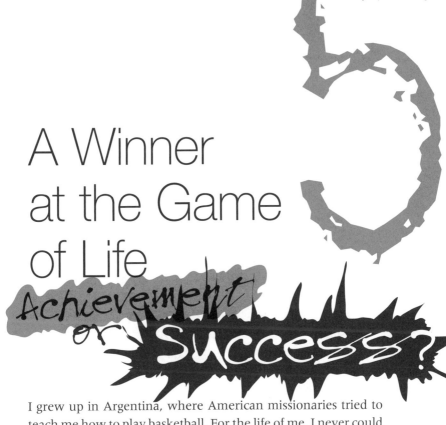

A Winner at the Game of Life

Achievement or Success?

I grew up in Argentina, where American missionaries tried to teach me how to play basketball. For the life of me, I never could figure out how to spin the ball so that when it hit the rim, it dropped through the hoop. Whenever I shot, the ball always spun *away* from the basket. Because I refused to make a fool of myself, I stopped playing basketball.

I stayed away from a lot of sports for that reason.

Why doesn't anyone want me on his team? And why don't I enjoy playing such sports? The fact is this: we love to win and hate to lose.

We love to win in athletics. We love to win in school. We love to win in love. We love to win, period. Why? Because we feel great when we win and depressed when we lose.

We love success. And why not? We're wired for it. God himself wants us to succeed. Before Joshua led the Israelites into the Promised Land, God gave his servant explicit instructions to help him "be successful" wherever he went and to make him "prosperous and successful" (Josh. 1:7–8 NIV).

Do you think the Lord wants anything less for us?

I look at it like this: What are your options? I see only three: success, mediocrity, or failure. Which do you pick?

I'll take success anytime—but not society's version.

The beautiful thing is that true success isn't about money. It does not mean beating the other guy. It does not mean surpassing your peers. It has to do with pleasing God and partnering with him in the greatest adventure in history.

Ephesians 2:10 teaches, "We are God's masterpiece. He has created us anew in Christ Jesus, so that we can do the good things he planned for us long ago." If we seek God's will, he will lead us to the works he has prepared. It could be graduating from an Ivy League college or becoming a medical missionary. It could mean becoming an evangelist and leading festivals or quietly making the most of every opportunity to serve others and share the gospel. The purpose isn't achievement for your own sake; it's succeeding at what God has prepared for you to do. If you accomplish what God wants, you are successful.

Choose Success, Not Achievement

It's only natural to desire success and to try to avoid failure. No one makes it a goal to fail as many times as possible.

And yet too often we settle for mere achievement when we could enjoy real success. You can achieve many things and yet wind up a spectacular failure. Since I prefer success, I try to keep in mind at least five ways that genuine success towers over mere achievement:

Achievement	Success
• Earns rewards	• Brings fulfillment
• Gains fame	• Wins respect
• Gratifies the flesh	• Makes the spirit content
• Meets goals	• Enjoys purpose
• Builds an empire	• Builds a legacy

Real success is finding God's will for your life and then doing it.

Earns Rewards vs. Brings Fulfillment

Hard work, perseverance, and determination can lead to great achievements that bring impressive rewards. Some young people spend all of their time chasing those rewards: valedictorian, captain of the team, star of the play, student body president, prom king or queen. Yet most of those who dedicate themselves to achievement eventually discover that the rewards and honors they worked so hard to earn don't satisfy for long.

True success, on the other hand, brings something that no material benefit can ever deliver: fulfillment. "The deepest, most satisfying delights God gives through creation are free gifts from nature and from loving relationships with people," says author John Piper. "After your basic needs are met, accumulated money begins to diminish your capacity for these pleasures rather than increase them. Buying things contributes absolutely nothing to the heart's capacity for joy."[1]

Author David G. Myers said it another way in his book *The American Paradox: Spiritual Hunger in an Age of Plenty.* "When sailing on the *Titanic*," he wrote, "even first class cannot get you where you want to go."[2] Observers saw the *Titanic* as quite an achievement when it sailed on its

Real success is finding God's will for your life and then doing it.

words or less

maiden voyage in April 1912, but it sank to the bottom of the frigid North Atlantic.

Achievement just will not get you where you want to go.

Commit to using your whole life for God—and start doing it—before the achievement trap tries to pull you away to other things.

God strongly desires that his people get the most out of life. Jesus said, "The thief's purpose is to steal and kill and destroy. My purpose is to give life in all its fullness" (John 10:10). God wants us to live such an abundant, successful life in the spiritual realm that it spills over into the physical realm. God wants to bless his people and put responsibility in their hands. He says to us, "I'm giving you this so that you can honorably use it for the extension of my kingdom" (see verses such as 2 Cor. 8:13–15).

Paul Jones was the lead singer for the pop group Manfred Mann in the 1960s. He set a lot of teen hearts on fire with tunes like "Do Wah Diddy Diddy." His good looks and versatility shot him to the top of the entertainment industry. In the early 1980s he co-starred with Fiona Hendley on a London stage. The two hit it off and soon moved in together.

Paul thought of himself as a brilliant debater, often using his wit and speaking skills to lampoon the beliefs of those he believed to be hypocritical Christians. For twenty-five years he considered himself a staunch atheist. And yet something kept bothering him.

His live-in girlfriend believed herself to be a Christian. "I was convinced that a Christian was somebody who believed there was a God, was pretty moral, was quite a good person, and probably went to church every now and again," Fiona said.[3] She grew up in a broken home and saw her mother seek relief in spiritualists and the occult. She herself tried to seek God through a cult. But none of it worked.

"I thought the way to escape all this pain was to make it in my career," she said. "I thought, *I'm going to do everything I can*

How do you know if you're being successful with your music?

I was taught early on never to believe my press, good or bad. Most of the time I'm able to gauge success through direct individual reactions to our music. This is why Kutless meets as many fans as possible and reads every email we receive.

Kyle Mitchell, Kutless

to be the best in what I can do, and I'm going to make it, and no one's going to get in my way, and no one's going to stop me."

One day, for some reason, Fiona walked into a church in central London. Even though she'd "sort of given up on God," she picked up a Bible, opened it, and read John 3:16: "For God so loved the world that he gave his one and only Son, that whoever believes in him shall not perish but have eternal life" (NIV).

"I was just absolutely astounded at this verse," she said, "because I thought, *If this is true, it's amazing and wonderful. If it's a lie, how dare it be written!*"

To see whether the verse might really be true, she and Paul started attending Sunday services and studying the Bible with a pastor. This both excited and frightened Fiona, because she thought, *Now hang on. If I follow this fully to find God, what happens if God takes something away from me that I want?* She wanted her

Who is one person you see as living a high definition life?

Mother Teresa definitely lived a high definition life. She was one person that just seized every moment and lived it for God and used it for truly loving people. I admire so much her servant's heart, her giving spirit, and her amazing love for God. Hers was a life that really inspired me. Also Billy Graham has definitely lived that kind of life. I am continually inspired by his integrity and by his consistency in his love for God and his passion to serve him.

Rebecca St. James

career more than anything and felt desperately afraid that God might send her to Africa instead. Paul, on the other hand, worried that he might have to stand up in front of a crowd someday and say, "Remember me? I'm a Christian now."

One day another early pop singer, Cliff Richard, phoned Paul and Fiona to ask them to come with him to one of my crusades. At first Paul hesitated, but when Cliff offered to buy dinner, the couple accepted. The message of Romans 1 struck home with both Paul and Fiona. Lost in a crowd of 16,000, Fiona said, "We felt like we were the only people there. It was like this spotlight was on us and we were kind of caught in the headlights."

At the invitation to receive Christ, Fiona got up to move to the front—but Paul grabbed her arm.

"Just a moment," he said. "Where are you going?"

"Well, it's time to stop with this half-baked stuff," she replied, "and Jesus is going to be my Lord from now on."

"That's terrific," Paul said. "Where am I sleeping tonight?"

Fiona sat back down. But before the night was up, both had committed their lives to Jesus Christ.

"I've just been so happy ever since," Fiona said. "The change is amazing. God has given me such a peace about that whole career thing. Now I have a purpose that I didn't have before."

Achievement or success? Paul and Fiona have had both, but they discovered that the first can't compare to the second.

Gains Fame vs. Wins Respect

Outstanding achievement can certainly get a person noticed. Who in our media-saturated culture hasn't heard the names of Tiger Woods, Julia Roberts, Oprah Winfrey, Stephen King, or Billy Graham? They have all excelled in their chosen fields of expertise and have in the process become household names.

But what, exactly, is fame worth? Mark Twain didn't think a whole lot of it. "Fame is a vapor; popularity an accident; the only earthly certainty is oblivion," he said.[4] Actress Marlo Thomas offered a less abstract critique: "Fame lost its appeal for me when I went into a public restroom and an autograph seeker handed me a pen and paper under the stall door."[5]

Achievement wins shaky fame that ebbs and flows according to changing public tastes, but success earns lasting respect.

I know a gentleman in Paraguay who will never be famous, but he has forever earned my respect. He volunteered several years ago to help out in the counseling ministry of one of our missions. We train local churches to counsel the hundreds who come seeking help for their marriages, families, and other personal problems. Even though this man was a pastor, he was very poor, had a shaggy appearance, and didn't read well. He sat in class all day, listening, as his twelve-year-old nephew took notes for him. A little exam followed the training. Again, the boy wrote for the pastor. This worried our director of counseling, but when he read the man's answers, he found them excellent.

A local church let us use its facility as a counseling center; about seventy counselors manned the place. One day all seventy were busy with counselees, while this humble brother sat there, awaiting his turn. In walked a well-dressed man—we learned he was a medical doctor—who said to the secretary at the door, "I need to talk to somebody. I have a problem with my wife. We're about to be divorced. With whom could I speak?"

Immediately the humble brother jumped up and said to the doctor, "I will counsel you," and the two left the room. About half an hour later they returned, arm-in-arm.

"Doctor, is there anything I can do for you?" our worried director of counseling asked when he caught sight of them.

"No, thank you," the doctor replied. "This gentleman has just helped me very well. I know what I must do when I get home. I just said a prayer and opened my heart to Christ." He then hugged the pastor and walked out.

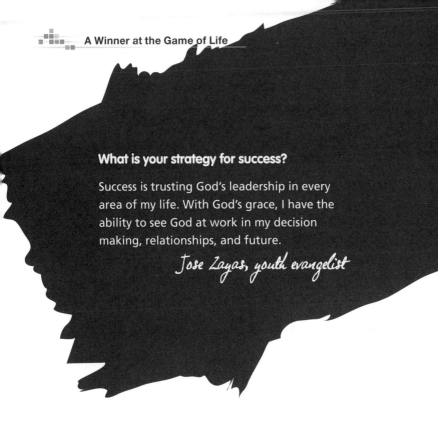

What is your strategy for success?

Success is trusting God's leadership in every area of my life. With God's grace, I have the ability to see God at work in my decision making, relationships, and future.

Jose Zayas, youth evangelist

The next day the place again was jammed, and there sat this pastor, waiting for another opportunity to counsel. The same doctor returned, this time with two of his colleagues.

"Doctor, could I give you a hand?" the counseling director asked. "Could I talk to you?"

"Thank you very much," the doctor replied, "but this brother here helped me to receive Christ yesterday. My two friends want to receive Christ too, and I want them to talk only to him."

So these three professionals headed into a classroom, led by the pastor, and the man led the other two doctors to Jesus Christ. The next day all three physicians showed up with a fourth doctor. All of them had serious marriage problems and knew one another from the country club. They insisted on talking to only one person. And the poor pastor with rumpled clothes led the fourth doctor to Jesus Christ.

After the mission, the four doctors got together with their wives and threw a big party. Whom do you think they invited? The evangelist whose name appeared on publicity posters all over town? They didn't even know me. Our counseling director? No, thank you. They asked the pastor and his nephew. Those professional men all became dedicated followers of Jesus Christ, became active in a local church, and put their families together again—thanks in large part to a poor, illiterate pastor. He'll never be famous, but do you think he's earned some respect? That man has enjoyed more success than 90 percent of all the Fortune 500 CEOs who ever lived.

Gratifies the Flesh vs. Makes the Spirit Content

Achievement feels good and gratifies our desire for victory, but the feeling never lasts. As I write, the playoffs are winding down in the National Basketball Association. In just a couple of weeks the league will crown a new champion. Although I'm no prophet, I can guarantee that one scene will occur just moments after the final buzzer. Some reporter will shove a microphone into the face of a jubilant athlete and ask something like, "Do you think you can repeat next year?"

The athlete will respond with some version of, "We just want to savor this for a while," but the damage already will have been done. Some portion of the winner's gratification will have vanished forever.

True success involves gratification, but it goes far beyond that to contentment. When you succeed at helping others overcome some persistent problem, you feel a contentment that just doesn't fade. When you succeed at the things that make God smile, the contentment you feel lasts and lasts. And that's true success.

Could you be missing out on this success? You don't lack for friends; you're a likable person; you live a good life. And yet, deep inside, you feel something's missing.

That "something" is the contentment only Jesus can bring, as Bruce Frydenlund can tell you. In fact, I'd like to let him do that, in his own words:

Driving down a Salt Lake City street in my beat-up Volkswagen van, broiling under the summer sun, I could see over the fence guarding an apartment complex courtyard. It was packed with young men and women having fun around a keg of beer and a very inviting swimming pool.

That's where I need to be, I thought. So I pulled over. The gate was locked, but it didn't take long to find an entrance through the laundry room. Trying my best to look like I belonged, I jumped into the pool.

But there was this guy checking people, asking, "Do you live here?" If not, he was kicking them out. When he came around, I'd go under water.

Then I started diving off the board. Back in North Dakota, I was in gymnastics, so diving was second nature to me. This guy swims over and says, "You dive pretty good. Would you mind teaching me?"

"Well, no . . . do you live here?" I asked.

"Why?"

"Could I be your guest?"

That's how I met Greg Connor, professional freestyle skier. One of the best in the country. We made a deal: I'd teach him diving, he'd teach me skiing. That's why I'd moved to Utah in the first place—skiing was at the top of the "good life" I desired.

Greg soon became my best friend, one of those few people whose heart connects with your own. We were roommates for five years. Then I moved to Portland, Oregon. He was in my wedding; I was in his. We'd visit in the summer. We called each other several times a month.

A few years ago Greg was going through some hard times. I advised Greg to resume exercising to help him shake off depression. Until recently, he had been running five miles a day.

"Bruce, I'm just kind of down," he said. "I try to run, but I get a side ache after about two blocks."

For two weeks I tried calling Greg every day because I'd never known him to be down and I felt concerned. But I couldn't reach him or his wife, Lori.

Finally on the Saturday before Thanksgiving when I called his home, his dad answered. And he dropped a bombshell!

"He's got cancer, Bruce. He's got only weeks to live."

This can't be, I thought. *Greg's a physical specimen: 6-foot-2, 210 pounds of muscle and bone. He's got legs as big as an oak. How can somebody like that have cancer?*

Since moving to Portland, I had committed my life to Jesus Christ and had been praying that Greg too would accept the Lord. Now, my prayers turned desperate. I pleaded with the Lord that he'd save Greg. And I asked the Lord over and over again to use me. Because Greg's my friend, and I wanted to be with him forever.

Then I braced myself to call my buddy in the hospital, where doctors hopelessly administered Greg's chemotherapy.

"Greg, is there anything I can do for you?" I asked.

"Send me something to read," he said.

Because I was sure Greg didn't have a Bible on his bookshelf, I went to a bookstore and bought one for him. I wrote in it, "This is the book that my mother read as she was dying. She went through a lot of pain, but she never seemed to suffer. Whatever she had, she found in here."

Over the next few weeks, I phoned Greg regularly and tried to arrange a trip to Salt Lake City. But Greg had a lot of friends who chipped together and bought Greg and Lori a trip to Hawaii. I felt frustrated because I knew I needed to see Greg soon.

The Bible says Christians should pray unceasingly. I had always thought, *That's ridiculous. How can we go around praying all the time?*

But for about a month, I was. Every time my mind went to Greg, I started praying. Nothing else seemed that important. What was important was getting to Greg.

After Hawaii, Greg went right back to the hospital for more chemotherapy. "Greg, I've gotta come see you," I said again.

This time God worked it out. A friend invited Greg and Lori to stay for a week at his duplex. "Come on up this weekend," Greg called to say. "We've got three days."

Where in your life have you experienced the greatest success?

Getting accepted to a study abroad program at Oxford University seemed like a huge success. But I soon realized that meeting my goal didn't equal success. Real success came by making the most of the experience, meeting new friends, enriching my life, and building a foundation to continue growing, learning, and accomplishing.

Rebekah Clark, editor

Just what I wanted to hear! But then I got nervous. I had never led anybody to the Lord. I knew I needed to, but I didn't know how. I asked my pastor, "What do I do?" And we went through the essential points of salvation. I kept praying, petitioning the Lord for Greg's soul.

A friend picked me up at the airport. "When you see Greg, he won't be the Greg you remember physically," Andy said. "But his spirit's there."

As I climbed the stairs at the duplex, I could hear Greg's voice. "Bruce, is that you?" I opened the door, and there was Greg lying on the couch. He was just a skeleton, maybe 85 pounds.

But when our eyes connected, this big smile came over his face. Andy was right—his spirit was there.

We talked for only a few minutes and then, taking his hand in mine, I said, "Greg, I don't know how to say this. You'll think I'm off the wall, but Greg, you gotta accept Jesus Christ."

"Yeah, I know," he said. "But I don't know how."

"Well, that's why I'm here."

Within fifteen minutes, Greg received Jesus Christ into his life. We read the Bible together awhile and then Greg fell asleep.

When Lori came home from work, we talked about Greg. "He's doing a lot better now," I said. When she asked why, I told her that he'd accepted Christ and explained how.

"Can I do that?" Lori asked. She accepted the Lord too!

I was home a few days when Greg's dad called with the news that Greg had died. He asked me to be a pallbearer.

Friends had a wake for Greg Connor, good Irish Catholic. And there, once again, was a keg of beer. Most of the people I knew from my hedonist days in Salt Lake City were there. Many of these friends had seen Greg the last day or two. Invariably they'd come up to me and ask, "What did you say to Greg?"

"Why?"

"Because he was so happy."

"All I did was share Jesus Christ with him," I got to say to at least fifteen, if not twenty, friends.

Jesus is the best gift I've ever received from God, followed by my wife and children. But right after them fits Greg. To think that God would use me to influence Greg for eternity—that too is an awesome gift from heaven.

Bruce's search for contentment began with athletic achievements. He thought that was what he wanted. But only in Jesus Christ did he—and his friend Greg—find true and lasting contentment.

The same is true for you. Other things might gratify for a while, but only Jesus can make you eternally content.

Meets Goals vs. Enjoys Purpose

You could hardly meet a young person who set and achieved more goals than Gary M. Hirte. He was twice named to an all-conference football team as a defensive lineman. Classmates voted him a member of the prom court. He earned his place as class salutatorian. He became his small town's first Eagle Scout in twenty years. So you might never have expected the next line as it appeared in the *Milwaukee Journal Sentinel*:

"It seemed Hirte, who turned 18 last month, succeeded at everything he tried—everything, authorities now say, except getting away with murder."[6]

In early 2004 the six-foot, five-inch senior at Weyauwega-Fremont High School in Wisconsin was charged with first-degree intentional homicide in the murder of Glenn Kopitske, a thirty-seven-year-old local eccentric with mental health issues. Police say Hirte bragged for months about killing the man by shooting him in the back of the head and then stabbing him three times. And why did he do it? Only to "see if he could get away with it," according to a secretly taped phone conversation.

"Why does someone who succeeds at everything he does want to do something like that?" asked Winnebago County Sheriff's Captain Steve Verwiel. "It's only speculation, but was it because he felt superior to all people? Or because it was the ultimate challenge?"

Hirte's story demonstrates that there is no benefit in meeting goals that don't serve a worthy purpose.

I meet many wealthy individuals who get excited to use their financial blessings for evangelism but never follow through. They have enjoyed incredible spiritual experiences, amazing business capacity, extensive education, a broad worldview—and yet they don't live to one-tenth of their full capacity. It's possible to go with the flow, not rock the boat, avoid great sins—just pursue the goal of being nice—and end up a failure.

I realize that not everybody can be a statesman or a politician or a public evangelist. But if we live with an eternal purpose rather than living to meet a few short-sighted goals, we are bound to work on the cutting edge. People will feel the touch of God when our lives touch theirs.

But woe to us if we're only meeting goals! Without an eternal purpose, meeting even great goals doesn't count for much in the end. To enjoy success at the highest level, you need an eternal purpose. Fortunately, that's just what Jesus Christ supplies.

Builds an Empire vs. Builds a Legacy

If you can travel to Asheville, North Carolina, visit the spectacular Biltmore Estate, a sprawling complex built by George W. Vanderbilt in the Blue Ridge Mountains. It features the largest house in the United States, its 250 rooms filled with fine art and period antiques.

One look at this impressive compound and you know that its builder controlled enormous assets and built mighty empires. Yet that same look reveals something else: nobody lives there anymore. The estate functions basically as a museum intended to draw gawking tourists.

Not much of a legacy, in my book. When I think of "homes" and "legacies," I can't help but think of my dad.

I love to visit Argentina, because each time I go there I get to hear new stories about him.

My dad built houses for nine couples whom he thought showed potential for starting local churches. He built a home for a couple I have met, and it's still in super shape. It boasts the same shiny, red roof tile my dad installed fifty-five years ago.

These folks told me that three weeks before my dad died, he came to the house and gave them the title to the property. "It's yours," he said. "You pay me any way you can. If you can't pay, that's all right, so long as you start a church in this town." And they did. The nine villages where my dad built homes all host active churches today. He maximized his potential in his own way, appropriate to his own style.

What's keeping you from maximizing your own potential? You may not have graduated from high school yet, but could it be that you're out to build an empire rather than leave a legacy?

A rich young power broker once approached the Lord Jesus and asked him anxiously, "Good Teacher, what should I do to get eternal life?" (Mark 10:17). The Gospel makes it clear that the man had youth, social standing, wealth, an attractive personality, sincerity, courage, humility, and religious training and that he led a clean life. Yet he felt desperate. Why?

It's not that he thought of himself as a bad person. Jesus didn't challenge him when he said he had kept God's commandments (Mark 10:18–21). It appeared this young man had everything going for him. Then why did he feel so desperate?

His problem was that he felt a desperate hunger for life. He was searching for satisfaction, for something more than an empire. He was searching for life with a capital *L*.

At that decisive moment, Jesus "felt genuine love for this man as he looked at him. 'You lack only one thing,' he told him. 'Go and sell all you have and give the money to the poor, and you will have treasure in heaven. Then come, follow me'" (10:21).

Jesus told the young man that he lacked only one thing. But what a thing to lack! If you lack that one thing, you lack everything.

Could it be that way with you? Everything seems all right. Your classes are going well. Your friends think you're great. Your parents trust you. Everything appears good—except one thing. You don't have Jesus Christ living in you. Listen, without his divine fuel, you may go on to build an empire, but you'll leave no legacy.

Jesus told the rich young man that only one thing stood in the way of his receiving eternal life. Only one idol blocked his access to God: money. So Jesus told him, chuck the idol and join me.

Do you know why many men and women lack assurance of eternal life? It is not because they are immoral or ungodly. It is because they have never taken the action that God demands. The Bible calls for action. You must *do* something. Jesus said to this young man, "Go, sell, give, come, and follow." Five simple commands. Jesus said, "I will give you eternal life and you can build a true legacy, if only you will just do what I say."

Life means making basic decisions. Do you know what happened to this young man—powerful, handsome, humble, rich, moral, and religious as he was? The Bible says he got up off his knees, dusted off his clothes, and walked away, greatly disappointed. He refused to do what Jesus asked of him, and he shuffled away, sad. And Jesus let him go.

He still lets young men and women walk away. During our festivals, in the midst of thousands of happy endings in which individuals settle their affairs with God, I've seen hundreds of "rich young power brokers" walk away sad. Many hear the voice of God, hear the demands of Jesus Christ, but respond, "I'm sorry, but I can't go through with it. I would rather build my empire than leave a legacy for God. I'm more concerned with what my friends and relatives think than what God thinks. I'm sorry." And they leave with their heads bowed and their faces sad.

Do not walk away like the rich young man! Don't leave lost and sad. Surrender to Jesus Christ. By faith say, "Lord God, I'm just like the rich young man. I feel a great emptiness inside. I will follow Christ. I trust him. I believe him."

When you accept Jesus's offer, the Bible says you become a king and priest (Rev. 1:6; 5:10). Through Jesus, you can begin to reign in life (Rom. 5:17; 2 Tim. 2:12; Rev. 20:6).

When you visit the poorest Christians in the world, such as those in the remotest villages of Guatemala or Bolivia, even illiterate believers can enter the room with dignity and confidence. Jesus Christ takes even those without shoes and causes them to walk with the bearing of kings and queens.

That's part of the legacy of Jesus Christ, and it far outdoes any human empire ever built.

Win or Lose

One afternoon years ago someone gave me tickets to the Wimbledon tennis championships. And it got me to thinking: *In life, as in tennis, there is no tie. You either win or you lose.*

Every one of us playing the game of life will end up as either winners or losers, depending on what we do with Jesus Christ. Are you going to be a winner? Or when it's all said and done, will you be a loser?

God wants us all to be winners. He made each one of us to enjoy life here and to wind up in God's Hall of Fame in heaven. So don't settle for mere achievement when you can enjoy true success. Jesus asked us, "How do you benefit if you gain the whole world but lose or forfeit your own soul in the process?" (see Luke 9:25). Don't give up your place in God's Hall of Fame. Choose success!

HOW TO BE Successful ACCORDING TO THE BIBLE

1. **Never set yourself up in opposition to God.**
   "Human plans, no matter how wise or well advised, cannot stand against the LORD" (Prov. 21:30).

2. **Make sure that you and God are walking the same path.**
   "David continued to succeed in everything he did, for the LORD was with him" (1 Sam. 18:14).

3. **See to it that both your methods and goals honor God.**
   "Uzziah sought God during the days of Zechariah, who instructed him in the fear of God. And as long as the king sought the LORD, God gave him success" (2 Chron. 26:5).

4. **Gain a thorough grasp of God's Word, the Bible.**
   "Study this Book of the Law continually. Meditate on it day and night so you may be sure to obey all that is written in it. Only then will you succeed" (Josh. 1:8).

5. **Pray for success.**
   "Please, LORD, please save us. Please, LORD, please give us success" (Ps. 118:25).

6. **Spend whatever time is necessary to gain whatever skills you may require.**

   "Since a dull ax requires great strength, sharpen the blade. That's the value of wisdom; it helps you succeed" (Eccles. 10:10).

7. **Seek out wise counselors and ask for their advice.**

   "Plans go wrong for lack of advice; many counselors bring success" (Prov. 15:22).

8. **Don't fly by the seat of your pants, but devise a plan.**

   "Good planning and hard work lead to prosperity, but hasty shortcuts lead to poverty" (Prov. 21:5).

9. **Commit your plans to the Lord.**

   "Commit your work to the LORD, and then your plans will succeed" (Prov. 16:3).

10. **Realize that God may have a different idea for your success than you do.**

    "You can make many plans, but the LORD's purpose will prevail" (Prov. 19:21).

WISE WORDS

[O GOD,] YOU WILL SHOW ME THE WAY OF LIFE, GRANTING ME THE JOY OF YOUR PRESENCE AND THE PLEASURES OF LIVING WITH YOU FOREVER.

King David of Israel,
Psalm 16:11

A Festival in Your Heart

Pleasure or Happiness?

For something that everybody says they desperately want, "happiness" sure has received some bad press over the years. Just listen to what some famous people of the past have said about happiness:

> Few people can be happy unless they hate some other person, nation, or creed.
>
> Bertrand Russell

> Happiness is not something you experience; it's something you remember.
>
> Oscar Levant

> I can sympathize with people's pains, but *not* with their pleasure. There is something curiously boring about somebody else's happiness.
>
> Aldous Huxley

How is it, I wonder, that something so appealing and attractive as happiness could generate such bad reviews? I'd be willing to bet that opinions as cynical as these spring into existence when someone who desperately wants happiness fails to get it.

The truth is, all of us want to be happy. All of us want to enjoy life, have fun, and take a heaping helping of the pleasures this world offers. I think psychologist Dr. Joyce Brothers is right on target when she writes, "True happiness is what makes life worthwhile. Yet happiness can be elusive—despite the fact that we seem to be wired for it."[1]

And why does happiness so often escape us? Anna Quindlen, a Pulitzer Prize–winning columnist and author of the book *A Short Guide to a Happy Life*, suggests that some of us miss out on happiness because we're just not looking. "I think a lot of us sleepwalk our way through our lives," she writes, "when, if we really opened our eyes, we would realize how much we were missing."[2]

The real question for us is, how can we open our eyes (and hearts) to genuine happiness? How can we step from a black and white world to one bursting with all the colors of the rainbow? Just how can we become truly happy?

Beware of Detours

Unfortunately, the road to happiness swarms with detours. Sometimes we miss out on true happiness because we get con-

25 words or less Simply put, pleasure feels good, but joy feels better.

fused about what it really is and therefore choose the wrong route. At other times we refuse to accept happiness when it pulls up alongside us. Sad to say, I think many Christians have rumbled down both of these bumpy highways.

One day my British friend Nigel Gordon and I stopped by an English pub for lunch. Over the fireplace in front of the bar hung a sign that read: "Good ale, good food, good times."

Man, I thought, *that sounds almost like Christians were meant to be.*

But never say any such thing to some Christians! Too often we give the impression that following Jesus Christ is a grim experience for which only the most somber, frowning, Secret Service–looking types qualify. Some of us almost refuse to have a good time.

How terrible that God offers us a fantastic way of life— beautiful, victorious, successful over sin, filled with the Holy Spirit and with the assurance of eternal life—and yet many of us don't really enjoy it.

Some time ago my wife was reading an old but classic book, *The God of All Comfort* by Hannah Whitall Smith. In her introduction Smith says she wrote the book because an agnostic fiercely challenged her faith. In essence he said, "Do you know why I will never consider God? It's because Christians, according to their religion, should have absolute joy and peace, happiness and victory. And yet they often look like the most miserable people in the whole world."[3]

Sadly, he hit too close to home.

Years ago we held a rally in a Western European city—one of the most miserable meetings ever. The music sounded like a funeral and a spirit of gloom filled the auditorium, yet some of the most distinguished evangelical leaders of that nation led the rally. I could not leave fast enough. When we drove away, none of us even wanted to stop for a Coke in that town.

When thirst got the better of us, however, we started looking for a restaurant. The only open establishment in the countryside

What brings you the greatest joy in life?

Without a doubt, skateboarding. When I'm on a skateboard, even when I'm just rolling, I have such a freedom. That is my worship to God—just like music or dancing. When I competed in the Tampa AM, I prayed before all of my runs and the Lord gave me the tricks to do. I find joy in worshiping God through skating.

Sierra Fellers, skateboard champion

was a pub, so we parked our car behind the building and went in. As soon as we walked through the doors, the patrons recognized our nationality and bellowed, "Welcome, Americans!" Someone was playing an accordion, others were banging and scratching on other instruments, smoke filled the place—and the people laughed and clapped and sang. They even offered us a free drink as honored foreigners. We accepted—a Coca-Cola.

What a contrast! I felt far happier in that bar than in the Christian meeting.

Who told us that uncomfortable clothes, serious faces, and worried expressions somehow qualify as more spiritual than being joyful and delighting in abundance? I cannot for the life of me figure it out. But perhaps it explains why a lot of people turn down Christianity—it seems to go against human nature's desire for happiness, and against what I believe God desires for us.

The Joyful Heart of God

"Can you imagine what it would be like if the God who ruled the world were not happy?" asks author John Piper. He continues:

> What if God were frustrated and despondent and gloomy and dismal and discontented and dejected? Could we join David and say, "O God, you are my God, earnestly I seek you; my soul thirsts for you, my body longs for you, in a dry and weary land where there is no water" (Ps. 63:1)? I don't think so. We would all relate to God like little children who have a frustrated, gloomy, dismal, discontented father. They can't enjoy him. They can only try not to bother him, and maybe try to work for him to earn some little favor.[4]

But that is not the God of the Bible! The God who reveals himself in the Scriptures overflows with joy. God is a good, loving, eternally happy God, an overflowing fountain of delight—and he wants the faces of his children to reflect his own infinite joy. It is no accident that Jesus Christ, who perfectly mirrors the very nature of God, loved to proclaim what he called "the Good News"—and the secret of the Good News is that life is meant to be *good*. Jesus offers us a joy-filled life, not a dull one.

C. S. Lewis once remarked, "Joy is the serious business of heaven." I think he meant that God passionately wants his people to enjoy life, to be happy and contented.

Lewis learned this from Jesus Christ, for in Matthew 7:11 the Savior says, "If you sinful people know how to give good gifts to your children, now much more will your heavenly Father give good gifts to those who ask him." Most parents want their kids to be happy. They want them to play and laugh and settle into a contented life. And according to Jesus, God wants this for us even more than parents want it for their kids.

Rejoice and Be Glad

It is not God's will that we shuffle miserably through life with gritted teeth, that we sweat buckets just to barely make it to heaven. It *is* God's purpose that, given the limitations of an imperfect world, his people celebrate and enjoy life. Consider just a few of the dozens of verses in the Bible that make this point:

> But let the godly rejoice.
> Let them be glad in God's presence.
> Let them be filled with joy.
>
> Psalm 68:3

> So I concluded that there is nothing better for people than to be happy and to enjoy themselves as long as they can. And people should eat and drink and enjoy the fruits of their labor, for these are gifts from God.
>
> Ecclesiastes 3:12–13

> Ask and you will receive, and your joy will be complete.
>
> John 16:24 NIV

> So I pray that God, who gives you hope, will keep you happy and full of peace.
>
> Romans 15:13

> Always be joyful.
>
> 1 Thessalonians 5:16

There's no way around it; the spiritual life is meant to radiate joy. The famous "fruit of the Spirit" passage in the fifth chapter of Galatians makes this very clear. Years ago on the radio I heard a woman read this passage, along with the final line: "Against such things there is no law." She then said something that encourages me to this day. "There is no law against too much love," she said. "There is no law against too much joy."

Such a simple thought, but it assures me that the serious business of heaven really is joy. Much of the Bible expresses this joyful element of the Good News. I wonder—when was the last time you cracked open a Bible to look for all the goodness God offers you?

If all your sins are forgiven; if your body is the temple of the Holy Spirit; if you have unlimited access to all of heaven's resources; if you have God's Word to guide you; if God promises never to leave you nor forsake you; if you're going to heaven when you die; if you'll live forever with a God who loves you—then shouldn't you be ecstatically happy?

The Holy Spirit tells believers to rejoice. When the Spirit of God comes to live within us, we gain the power to enjoy life even in bad times. Of course, troubles will come. But we can remain happy in the Lord even in the middle of terrible circumstances. Every believer has the power to make this choice because the Holy Spirit, the source of all joy, lives within every believer (see Rom. 8:9).

The Biggest Detour of All

I believe pleasure can become one of the biggest detours to true happiness. While we all want to be happy—truly happy—too often we settle for mere pleasure. We enjoy moments of delight, but satisfying and lasting happiness (what the Bible calls joy) escapes us.

And just how can pleasure get in the way of joy? It's not that pleasure's bad and joy's good. Don't think for a moment that I'm criticizing pleasure! God himself says he wants to fill us with joy in his presence, with "eternal pleasures" at his right hand.

But while pleasure stimulates the senses, joy satisfies the soul. Pleasure comes from the outside; joy flows from within. Pleasure vanishes in the presence of pain; joy can sustain a person even in great sorrow.

I think true happiness surpasses mere pleasure in at least five important ways:

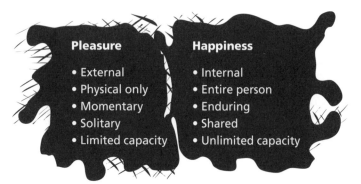

Pleasure

- External
- Physical only
- Momentary
- Solitary
- Limited capacity

Happiness

- Internal
- Entire person
- Enduring
- Shared
- Unlimited capacity

Simply put, pleasure feels good, but joy feels better.

External vs. Internal

We feel pleasure when some outside source delights one or more of our five senses. We take pleasure in the fragrance of a rose, the fur of a puppy, the slick outline of a Porsche, the delicious taste of a fresh cherry pie. God has designed our bodies to enjoy the pleasures of his creation.

But happiness doesn't have to depend on outside sources to thrive. We can experience a deep kind of joy that bubbles up from the inside. Genuine happiness comes from inside, not from the outside.

How is this possible? Jesus said, "If you believe in me, come and drink! For the Scriptures declare that rivers of living water will flow out from within" (John 7:38). Notice: not from outside, but from inside! The Gospel writer leaves us no doubt about what Jesus intended by his metaphor, for he adds, "When he said 'living water,' he was speaking of the Spirit, who would be given to everyone believing in him" (v. 39).

For good reason the Bible continually connects joy with the Spirit of God. Jesus was "filled with the joy of the Holy Spirit" (Luke 10:21). The disciples were "filled with joy and with the Holy Spirit" (Acts 13:52). The kingdom of God is a matter of "joy in the Holy Spirit" (Rom. 14:17). And even despite "severe suffering," it is possible to overflow "with joy from the Holy Spirit" (1 Thess. 1:6).

I saw this amazing truth in action a few years ago on a trip to the former Soviet Union. Viktor Hamm, my excellent interpreter, described how Josef Stalin had sentenced Viktor's father to a Siberian prison camp as punishment for expressing his faith.

The elder Mr. Hamm and the other prisoners in the enormous gulag worked every day in a mine. Each morning they'd stand in line to receive their picks and shovels, and every evening they'd return to hand in their equipment. Soon Mr. Hamm began to pray, "Lord, there has to be a Christian somewhere in this camp. Help me to find him, someone with whom I can pray."

One day he thought he recognized a certain look about the man who handed out the mining equipment. "I think he's a Christian," he said to himself. But he thought, *How shall I approach him without giving myself away? If he's KGB, I'm finished. But let's see who he is.*

With joy and fear rising at the same time in his heart, he said to the man, "You know, they expect us to achieve our goals, but they don't give us the water and the straw to get the job done."

Anyone familiar with the Bible would recognize the reference to Moses and the days of Hebrew slavery in Egypt. The worker looked at Mr. Hamm for a moment and then said slowly, "Wait a minute. Stand here." When all the other men left he asked, "Why did you mention the straw and the water? Where did you get that?"

"Oh, I read about it in a pretty good Book," replied Mr. Hamm, trying hard to keep from trembling.

"Yes, I think I read that Book too," said the man. Then he paused. "I notice that you don't swear like the other men. They are always fighting, but you don't get into that sort of thing. Why is that?"

"My Father won't let me."

The conversation paused again. As the man carefully looked Mr. Hamm up and down, he finally asked, "Your Father wouldn't be my Father, would he?"

"My Father has only one Son," said Mr. Hamm, getting excited.

"My Father has only one Son too," replied the man.

"Believer?"

"Believer!"

And with great joy despite their miserable surroundings, they began to pray in secret. But their prayer times didn't stay secret for long; their joy just wouldn't allow it. Joy has a strong tendency to reproduce itself in others. By the time the pair were set free, *three hundred* prisoners had come to follow Jesus Christ.

Josef Stalin might have been able to deprive millions of prisoners of any kind of pleasure, but he had no power to shut out their joy. When a river of joy flows from deep inside, nothing can stop the rushing current. Joy continues to bloom even when evil men try to blot out the sun.

The Old Testament compares joy with an overflowing cup. The psalmist said to God, "You welcome me as a guest, anointing my head with oil. My cup overflows with blessings" (Ps. 23:5). This prompts an important question: Is your cup overflowing? Are you fueled with the Holy Spirit *now*? Don't neglect the huge inner treasure you have through the fullness of the Holy Spirit.[5]

Physical Only vs. Entire Person

Your five senses provide the main channel to physical pleasure. When your nerve endings sense certain kinds of stimuli, they send electrical pulses to your brain, which interprets them as pleasurable. Most pleasure is a sensory experience. Joy, on the other hand, involves far more than the body. This kind of rich happiness reaches down into your soul and extends up to the spirit. Happiness and joy can thrive even in the absence of pleasant physical stimuli.

Those who want happiness need something deeper than the excitement of their physical senses. They need a mission in life. If someone told you tomorrow morning that you had only a year to live, would you change how you're living today? And if you would, doesn't that suggest that you should rethink how you're living today?

A few years ago, one of my nephews (I'll call him Kenneth) was near death. He had AIDS. During a family reunion, Kenneth and I broke away for a walk. He looked like a hollow shell, laboring for breath.

"Kenneth, you know you're going to die any day," I said. "Do you have eternal life?"

"Luis," he replied, "I know God has forgiven me and I'm going to heaven."

As we put our arms around each other and prayed and talked some more, I became convinced that Jesus had forgiven Kenneth. Several short months later, he went to be with the Lord at age twenty-five. And now, through his death, he encourages young people to find and follow a greater mission in life than merely seeking physical pleasure.

Momentary vs. Enduring

Pleasure lasts only so long as the brain continues to receive signals that the mind interprets as pleasurable. Shortly after the signals end, so does the sensation of pleasure. That's why you can eat a double scoop of triple chocolate ice cream one moment and crave another double scoop thirty seconds later. The pleasure remains only so long as it lasts. It's great but momentary.

How do you see the difference between pleasure and joy?

Pleasure is cotton candy. It's delicious for a moment, but dissolves in seconds. Joy is an everlasting gobstopper. The flavor lasts and lasts. Sometimes, you may even forget it's in your mouth, but you can count on it being there. Because joy isn't affected by external circumstances, we can have joy even when life seems to have lost its sweetness.

Rebekah Clark, editor

Real joy, on the other hand, lasts and lasts. True happiness radiates from the core of your being. Dr. Joyce Brothers comes close to the biblical idea here when she writes, "Happiness comes down to being quietly content most of the time."[6] Think of joy as an inner, lasting contentment. As one scholar notes, the Bible pictures joy not merely as an emotion but as "a characteristic of the Christian."[7]

God is delighted when his children live with joy and contentment. If we keep our consciences clear, the Lord wants us to feel happy, even if we're not naturally the giddy type. Believers ought to rejoice in the Lord over the good things he brings their way. "Yes, the LORD has done amazing things for us! What joy!" said the psalmist (Ps. 126:3).

Unfortunately, some of us tend to lose our joy. Sometimes we lose it by focusing on unpleasant events. Sometimes we lose it by forgetting the spiritual riches that Jesus has given us. And sometimes we lose it because we confuse pleasure with joy.

Those who make this mistake believe happiness comes only rarely and leaves with the speed of light. To look at their faces, you'd swear God never sent his Son into the world. They remind me a whole lot more of a woman named Jana than of Jesus.

I met Jana just before the dismantling of the Soviet Union. This Russian news reporter scheduled an interview with me as we prepared for a crusade in Leningrad. Over lunch she looked at me with weary eyes and muttered, "You seem so peaceful and happy."

"Oh?" I replied, "Does it show? Well, I *am* peaceful and I *am* happy."

We dropped the subject almost immediately and continued the interview, but by the end of our time together she looked so *un*happy that I said, "You know, Jana, you look so unpeaceful and unhappy."

"Of course I'm unhappy," she snapped. "We atheists, we're never happy."

I've never been able to forget her words. A few days later, at a crusade in Riga, I quoted Jana and said to the crowd, "You atheists, you're so unhappy."

To my surprise, the Russians enthusiastically responded in chorus, "*Da, da!*" "Yes, yes!"

When a few minutes later I gave an invitation to receive Jesus Christ, it seemed as though half the crowd came forward, hoping to find joy in Jesus Christ. I could hardly believe it.

Still, I have a harder time believing that many of those who already *have* found Jesus Christ *still* search for joy. Do you? Maybe you never learned to tap the unlimited resources to which you're entitled in Christ. Perhaps you feel miserable, not because Jesus Christ has failed to keep up his end of the bargain but because you confuse praying a prayer for salvation with a vital, growing relationship with Jesus. The two are not the same! You can't have the second without the first, but you certainly can have the first and still not have the second. Conversion to Christ does not guarantee a life of joy, but it does open the door to it. As I said, you must choose to enter.

If you've lost the thrill and freshness of the gospel, you need to do a personal check-up. If you're bored, realize that you're bored with Jesus Christ. The solution? Share Jesus Christ with others. "I pray that you may be active in sharing your faith," the apostle Paul wrote, "so that you will have a full understanding of every good thing we have in Christ" (Philem. 6 NIV). Give out the Good News and you'll appreciate it in a fresh way yourself.

Solitary vs. Shared

Pleasure is intensely personal. No one can taste that Swiss chocolate sliding down my throat but me. Nobody but me can feel the tension disappear as strong fingers work my neck.

Since joy isn't confined to the physical world, however, it can be shared in ways that rise far above sensual pleasure. True happiness finds its fullest expression in community.

I believe this is a major reason Jesus Christ founded and blessed the church. He knew that "on earth" we would "have many trials and sorrows" (John 16:33). So he commanded his followers to love one another, going so far as to say, "Your love for one another will prove to the world that you are my disciples" (John 13:35). He created the church as a place of healing, rest, strength, and joy. In the church he wants us to "think of ways to encourage one another to outbursts of love and good deeds," and he advises us to "not neglect our meeting together, as some people do, but encourage and warn each other" (Heb. 10:24–25).

The church Jesus envisioned is a joyful place! It ought to make people feel at home. It should proclaim that the Creator meant life to be enjoyed.

A few years ago I met with Rick Warren, senior pastor of Saddleback Church in Lake Forest, California, and author of the best-seller *The Purpose-Driven Life*. My wife and I and a few members of my team ate dinner with him and discussed the festival concept we've used in communities across the nation. I marveled at this busy pastor's friendly spirit, genuine enthusiasm, and joy in Jesus Christ. He lit up as we explained what we were trying to accomplish.

Man, I thought, *this pastor is enjoying the Christian life to the full. Why can't all Christians follow his lead?* I couldn't help but think, *This is the way it was meant to be. You're contented and at peace and happy to meet somebody. You chat together and you eat and you laugh. And God is at the center of everything.*

How can a person who does not feel happy in the Lord bless other people? Sure, God can use anyone who communicates his truth—but if you want your *life* to bring happiness to others, you had better be a person filled with the Holy Spirit, whose fruit is joy.

The amazing message of Jesus Christ deserves to be declared to everyone who has ears to hear. The happiness it brings cannot be imprisoned but insists on breaking out to bless more and more people. The church, at its best, brings believers together for encouragement, instruction, worship, and service. And the result, by God's grace, is overflowing joy.[8]

Limited vs. Unlimited

There are limits to most physical pleasure. When you exceed certain boundaries, you perceive further stimulation as pain. With pleasure, there really is such a thing as too much of a good thing.

Eat too much pastry, you get sick. Stay in the sun too long, you get burned. Listen too long to loud music, you go deaf. Overindulge in any normally fun activity, from eating to sailing, and at some point you'll cross the line into pain.

If there exists a similar "threshold of pain" for joy, however, I have yet to find it. So far as I can tell, *nothing* limits the amount of joy one person can experience. "Limits" and "joy" simply do not go together. They live in entirely different neighborhoods, speak entirely different languages.

I've noticed, though, that while most people recognize the limits to pleasure, they see no such limits to unhappiness. Many of these people give up on life, sentence themselves to prison, then slam and lock the cell door.

Thousands of students wake up every morning and wish they could fall asleep again. Millions of people take Valium or Prozac just to keep from having to deal with a disappointing life. Don't let it happen to you! You might feel full of life right now, but without Christ supplying you with a daily ration of joy, things can quickly turn sour.

A friend of mine, an elder in our church, went to visit a woman whom he had known as a teenager. He made the trip

How do you see pleasure getting in the way of true joy for people today?

No one enjoys problems and challenges. We'd prefer that life was easy and fun. But I've learned that running after pleasure to avoid pain makes me miss out on the joy that comes from watching God turn awful situations into amazing opportunities.

Ann-Margret Hovsepian, author

at the urging of the woman's sister, who warned him, "She's in really bad shape."

Barry said that his old friend looked unbelievably miserable, sad, and discouraged. "Where's the young girl I used to know twenty years ago?" he asked. "You were so happy, so free. What's happened to you?"

"Forget it," she said. "I'm like a zombie now. I sit here smoking my cigarettes, watching my television."

Humanly speaking, the woman had plenty of reason for discouragement. Her alcoholic husband kept a steady job, but he never showed her the tiniest ounce of love. The only thing she knew about marriage was that it hurt and kept on hurting. She felt lonely and empty and worthless. With her youth gone and no spiritual resources to draw on, any happiness she ever knew had dwindled to a memory. The limits to pleasure, she knew. But an endless capacity for joy? That she could not even imagine.

Maybe, even as a teenager, you find yourself in the same boat. You used to feel happy. But now you feel no joy, no happiness, no delight in God. Where has all the happiness gone? *Something* happened. Maybe you got trapped in unhealthy habits of drug or alcohol abuse. Maybe you got involved with "the wrong crowd." Maybe you moved away from your hometown and haven't been able to fit in where you are. Or maybe it was something else. But something has gone wrong.

The Lord Jesus says to you, "I want your joy to be complete. I want you to experience the kind of deep contentment that can fill you with delight regardless of your circumstances. I want you to enjoy the rich happiness that comes from knowing I love you with my whole heart."

If you feel alone, empty, and confused; if you haven't felt happy for a long time—then open your heart to the Lord Jesus. Say, "Lord Jesus, come into my heart. Despite my problems, be real to me. Lord, be my Savior, my Friend, my God." Discover for yourself that his joy has no limits.

Can Unbelievers Feel Happy?

But maybe you have a question. "Do you mean that people can never experience true happiness without having Jesus Christ as their Savior?" you ask. "Because if that's your message, I don't buy it. I know plenty of non-Christians who seem pretty happy to me."

Actually, so do I. The Bible declares that even those who have no relationship to Jesus can still enjoy a certain type of happiness. The apostle Paul told the citizens in the ancient city of Lystra that God had always given them "reminders" of his love by giving them "joyful hearts" (Acts 14:17). That wasn't phony joy or counterfeit joy. Still, they didn't have the full kind of joy available only to those in whom the Spirit of God lives.

I tried to make this clear during a radio interview I did in 1998 on the BBC's *Five Live* program. The show's host, Nicki, asked me if people could be "truly happy if Jesus is not in their lives." I suggested they could not. I said someone might have "money in your pocket, and your body's in shape this week, but the inner core—the spirit, the inner person—is never fulfilled without Jesus Christ. . . . If you don't know God, a third of your personality remains empty, dead."

Nicki then invited non-Christian listeners to call in if they considered themselves truly happy.

A caller named Norman disagreed with me. "I was slightly appalled by his statement that nobody can be truly happy if you do not believe or have Jesus in your life," he said. "I think that's the biggest lot of nonsense I've heard in my life. I'm not a particularly religious person, but in my life I am truly happy. I'm married, I have two children, I'm healthy, my wife's healthy, my children are healthy, and we have no financial problems. We are truly happy in every sense."

"Norman, look," I replied, "you are missing out on one-third of your life. You are happy on the physical dimension. You are happy on the soul dimension—intellect, emotions, and will. But what about your spirit, Norman? You're missing out there. I'm glad you're happy, and I never claim that non-Christians can't experience some measure of true happiness—but you cannot be *fully* happy till your spirit lives."

We exchanged a few more comments, then I said, "Norman, one question. A serious question. I was in Bristol last year, and an attorney, just your age, had two little kids. His little girl died. He did not go to church, didn't believe in Jesus. He was absolutely devastated because he had no idea: *Where did she go? Where am I going? Will I ever see her again?* That's the spiritual, eternal dimension. Norman, you've got to give it time. Right now, you're happy, your body's in shape, your kids are great. But what about eternity, buddy?"

My radio friend had an answer for that. "I believe that when we die, we do not die," Norman said. "I believe we go somewhere else. I have relatives and close family members who have died, and I take solace in the fact that I don't believe that this is the only place where we exist. But that doesn't mean I believe in Jesus. I believe that this isn't the only planet we go to. We will all go somewhere, eventually."

On what did Norman base his hope? He didn't say. What specifics could he give about his hope? He didn't clarify. In blind faith he simply declared that somewhere in this vast universe there is a planet (apparently) to which the dead somehow transport themselves. What sort of conditions exist on that world? What do the inhabitants do? Where are they headed? These and a thousand other questions Norman left hanging.

I admire Norman for his ability to find hope and "solace" in such an apparently groundless belief, but I confess I find no hope in it. And certainly no joy. His comments convinced me more than ever that while we may feel happy on the level of the physical and the soul, until we ask God to breathe life into our spirits, we can never be happy on the largest of the three levels. And therefore we will never enjoy the promise of Jesus: "You will be filled with my joy. Yes, your joy will overflow!" (John 15:11).

The Lord created us to be happy, to enjoy a festival in our heart, and through Jesus Christ he has offered to give us a bottomless capacity for joy. He speaks promise after promise of blessing, assuring us of joy in his presence and eternal pleasures at his right hand.

The truth is, God does not want anyone to miss out on the party he plans to throw for us in heaven.

So why miss it?

HOW TO BE Happy
ACCORDING TO THE BIBLE

1. Believe in God.
"He and his entire household rejoiced because they all believed in God" (Acts 16:34).

2. Trust in God.
"So I pray that God, who gives you hope, will keep you happy and full of peace as you believe in him" (Rom. 15:13).

3. Embrace the salvation God offers.
"You love him [Jesus] even though you have never seen him. Though you do not see him, you trust him; and even now you are happy with a glorious, inexpressible joy. Your reward for trusting him will be the salvation of your souls" (1 Peter 1:8–9).

4. Don't be passive about your happiness, but work toward it.
"We want to work together with you so you will be full of joy as you stand firm in your faith" (2 Cor. 1:24).

5. Ask Jesus to meet your needs.
"The truth is, you can go directly to the Father and ask him, and he will grant your request because you use my name. You haven't done this before. Ask, using my name, and you will receive, and you will have abundant joy" (John 16:23–24).

6. Become familiar with Jesus's promises.
"I have told them many things while I was with them so they would be filled with my joy" (John 17:13).

7. Express your love for Jesus Christ by obeying him.
"When you obey me, you remain in my love, just as I obey my Father and remain in his love. I have told you this so that you will be filled with my joy. Yes, your joy will overflow!" (John 15:10–11).

8. **Don't be a loner, but spend time with other believers.**

   "I will continue with you so that you will grow and experience the joy of your faith. Then when I return to you, you will have even more reason to boast about what Christ Jesus has done for me" (Phil. 1:25–26).

9. **When life gets hard, remember the rewards God has in store for you.**

   "You suffered along with those who were thrown into jail. When all you owned was taken from you, you accepted it with joy. You knew you had better things waiting for you in eternity" (Heb. 10:34).

   "Though our bodies are dying, our spirits are being renewed every day. For our present troubles are quite small and won't last very long. Yet they produce for us an immeasurably great glory that will last forever!" (2 Cor. 4:16–17).

10. **Accept your lot in life and remember that happiness is a gift of God.**

   "And it is a good thing to receive wealth from God and the good health to enjoy it. To enjoy your work and accept your lot in life—that is indeed a gift from God" (Eccles. 5:19).

WISE WORDS

DON'T WORRY ABOUT ANYTHING; INSTEAD, PRAY ABOUT EVERYTHING. TELL GOD WHAT YOU NEED, AND THANK HIM FOR ALL HE HAS DONE. IF YOU DO THIS, YOU WILL EXPERIENCE GOD'S PEACE, WHICH IS FAR MORE WONDERFUL THAN THE HUMAN MIND CAN UNDERSTAND. HIS PEACE WILL GUARD YOUR HEARTS AND MINDS AS YOU LIVE IN CHRIST JESUS.

the apostle Paul,
Philippians 4:6

A Priceless Gift
That Costs Us
Nothing

Relief or Peace?

Comedian and late-night talk show host Jay Leno once suggested how he might try to impress the judges if he were somehow to compete at a famous beauty pageant: "As Miss America, my goal is to bring peace to the entire world and then to get my own apartment."[1]

We laugh at the absurdity, but sometimes apartments are just what one needs to get peace—if not world peace, then at least some personal peace. We long for tranquility, quiet, harmony, serenity, and calm. Unfortunately, it just doesn't seem easy to find.

Peace is one of the tremendous benefits of coming to know Jesus Christ. When you find peace with God, you gain peace with others, and you begin to experience great peace in your soul—the amazing peace of God. You learn how to put aside the tension and turmoil and unrest that once bothered you and replace it with a quiet confidence. Your peace bubbles up from within, out of a calm spirit energized by the living God.

Peace or Relief?

We all want peace, but in a world so torn apart by hatred and unrest, it's easy to mistake genuine peace for an attractive counterfeit or to rely on a less effective alternative. And we have many of both to choose from!

Every day many of us settle for counterfeit peace without even knowing it. We convince ourselves that peace comes through lots of activity, academic or athletic honors, the newest fashions, joining the "right" cliques, or "spiritual" activities. Some of us, feeling certain that it's just not possible to find real peace, seek out simple relief. So we run from a good part of our pain through the use of alcohol, drugs, sex, or a party mentality. Relief may not be peace, but it feels better than stress or pain.

It seems to me, however, that we all need to ask a basic question: Does genuine peace really exist? And if so, can we find it and get it for ourselves? Is it possible to leave behind the weak option of relief to enjoy the wonderful advantages of peace?

Not only is it possible, but I maintain that millions of believers throughout the ages and across the globe have come to understand personally that "The LORD gives his people strength. The LORD blesses them with peace" (Ps. 29:11).

Real peace—the kind that God places in the hearts of his children—is better than mere relief in at least five ways:

Relief	Peace
• Comes and goes	• Remains steady
• Dulls anxiety	• Lends quiet confidence
• Delivered from outside	• Drawn from inside
• Requires increasing dosages	• Enjoys growing calm
• Expensive	• Priceless

It saddens me that so many of us settle for relief when what we really want, what we really need, is peace. Sex or solitude, ecstasy or excess can bring some relief—but why settle for a mere hiccup of serenity when God offers you a huge lungful of inner calm? Why not instead choose real, genuine, personal peace?

Comes and Goes vs. Remains Steady

Relief comes and goes. The pain subsides only so long as we feel distracted by something else. But as soon as that distraction ceases, the pain returns—and quite possibly with greater intensity than before. The peace of God, however, remains steady and firm regardless of circumstances. Why? Because the infinite God supplies it: "You will keep in perfect peace all who trust in you, whose thoughts are fixed on you!" (Isa. 26:3).

Nothing can take away a growing Christian's peace *if* the Christian chooses to trust God. Though circumstances may shake you up, no outside force can strip away your peace. What if you fail a big midterm? What if you're mugged? What if your doctor tells you that he's sorry, but you have an inoperable form of cancer? Those things naturally cause a lot of anxiety, but believers who keep their minds focused on the solid rock of Jesus Christ can (and often do) say things like, "Lord, this could be a great opportunity to tell others about you."

On April 20, 2001, missionary Jim Bowers lost his wife, Veronica "Roni" Bowers, and their newly adopted seven-month-old daughter, Charity, in a terrifying tragedy. As the Bowers flew to their post on the Amazon River, a Peruvian Air Force jet mistook their plane for a drug-trafficking vessel and opened fire. A single bullet instantly killed both Veronica and Charity. Jim, his son Cory, and the pilot survived the

Counterfeit peace can bring some relief—but why settle for a mere hiccup of serenity when God offers you a huge lungful of inner calm?

words or less

What Scripture is the most helpful for you in seeking peace for your life?

Psalm 46:1-2, which says, "God is our refuge and strength, an ever-present help in trouble. Therefore we will not fear, though the earth give way and the mountains fall into the heart of the sea" (NIV). These verses remind me that no matter what happens, from natural disasters to the challenging trials of life, God never changes. His constancy is my strength when everything else fails.

Elizabeth Ries Jones, author and editor

crash into the Amazon River but had to recover Veronica and Charity's bodies.

When memorial services for his loved ones received international media coverage, Jim did not express bitterness or a desire for revenge; instead, he glorified God. "Obviously it hurts," he said, "but God works mysteriously to give me comfort so that I don't have to be sad all the time. . . . One sign that God was responsible for what happened is . . . the effect on missionary work now. I'm hoping it will result in an increase in missionaries in the future. I'm sure it will; people are challenged now to go do what Roni did. . . . Cory and I are experiencing an inexplicable peace, and to me, that's proof that God is in this."[2]

The peace of God doesn't mean that you feel no terror or pain when horrifying circumstances strike; it simply means that God's peace can overwhelm anything thrown at it from the outside. No outside force can take away the Christian's peace. Not your school. Not your teacher. Not even your brothers or sisters! Only two things can rob a Christian of God's peace: lack of trust in the Savior and unconfessed sin.

In 2 Thessalonians 3:16 the apostle Paul wrote, "May the Lord of peace himself always give you his peace no matter what happens. The Lord be with you all." When Paul ended with, "The Lord be with you all," he wasn't just trying to sound spiritual. He meant that his friends needed to depend on God and consciously make him part of their day-to-day lives. Only then could they expect to enjoy God's peace.

And don't be fooled: while God offers us all the resources we need to enjoy his peace, many of us never take him up on his offer. Why not? Because we try to fix things by ourselves. Or we choose the brief pleasures of some favorite sin. We forget that the Lord tells us, "If your sinful nature controls your mind, there is death. But if the Holy Spirit controls your mind, there is life and peace" (Rom. 8:6).

Do you want God's Holy Spirit to flood your mind and heart with his amazing peace? Do you want to free yourself from continual inner turmoil? You really can have God's peace if you want it. Isaiah says that Jesus "was wounded and crushed for our sins. He was beaten that we might have peace" (53:5). When Jesus took the punishment that our sins deserved, he made peace possible between us and our holy God. All it takes for you to receive his peace is to commit your life to Jesus Christ through faith.

And yet, even those who know and love Jesus Christ—even those who make Jesus a daily part of their lives—even *they* can be rocked by tragedy and hardship. The peace of God doesn't shield any of us from life's unpleasant moments, like some sort of supersedative. God's peace doesn't make faithful believers to march through life with vacant eyes and frozen smiles. But it does give them a confidence and calmness of spirit that allows them to deal with whatever comes their way.

For the longest time my wife could not understand why I harped on the Bible's picture of human beings as creatures with body, soul, and spirit (1 Thess. 5:23; Heb. 4:12 NIV). "So what?" she'd ask. "How does that knowledge help anyone?"

Then she got cancer, had major surgery, and started chemotherapy. "You know, at last I understand the value of your hammering home that business about body, soul, and spirit," she told me. "My body is in pain and I'm not sure whether I care much for it. My spirit is absolutely at peace. I'm ready to die, though I don't want to die; I really want to see our sons grow up. Still, I'm ready. I'm at peace. I have no fear. At the same time, however, my soul is a yo-yo. One day I wake up and I'm happy because I'm alive. Another day I wake up and I feel depressed because the cancer could have spread undetected."

That's the reality we all have to face. The peace of God doesn't mean the absence of concern. So then, are Christians lying when they say, "I have absolute peace with God, although I can't stop wondering if the cancer could be in my liver"? Not at all. To say such a thing simply means that the one speaking is a complete human being with body, soul, and spirit. Even when we belong to God, our emotions go up and down and our feelings teeter-totter.

- The *body* is hurting and sick (it's going to die anyway)
- The *spirit* is utterly at peace (secure and assured of eternity)
- The *soul* will fluctuate emotionally, depending on circumstances (and one day it too will be completely redeemed)

So long as we live in these disintegrating bodies, our emotions tend to skitter up and down depending on circumstances. Without God, those emotions take control and quickly put us in chains of fear and anxiety. But with God, the peace we enjoy in our spirit greatly influences the fluctuating emotions of our soul. You do not have to be ruled by your roller-coaster feelings.

Dulls Anxiety vs. Lends Quiet Confidence

No fortune ever built and no alcoholic beverage ever brewed has ever eliminated the anxiety felt by a worried human being. The best those things can do is dull the pain for a little while. They can briefly take the edge off the knife, but in the end they often wind up sharpening the blade to a razor's edge.

Peace, on the other hand, means not so much the absence of anxiety as the presence of quiet confidence. It is "God's holy presence in every experience of our human existence."[3]

Quiet confidence naturally grows in the heart of an individual who lives in the peace of God. "The fruit of righteousness will be peace," said Isaiah; "the effect of righteousness will be quietness and confidence forever" (32:17 NIV). Those who live deeply in the peace of God believe God when he says, "You need not be afraid of disaster or the destruction that comes upon the wicked, for the LORD is your security. He will keep your foot from being caught in a trap" (Prov. 3:25–26).

I saw the peace of God at work in an amazing way in my mother. She became a widow at age thirty-four, quickly lost the family business, and had to find a way to feed seven children on almost nothing. Yet to my eyes she seemed to survive on two verses from the lips of Jesus: "I have told you all this so that you may have peace in me. Here on earth you will have many trials and sorrows. But take heart, because I have overcome the world" (John 16:33) and "I am leaving you with a gift—peace of mind and heart. And the peace I give isn't like the peace the world gives. So don't be troubled or afraid" (John 14:27).

Mom never let our extreme poverty get to her. While she didn't enjoy our circumstances and did what she could to improve our situation, I still remember the warm smile that overflowed from the depths of a heart at perfect peace.

God's peace does far more than dull anxiety. It lends a quiet confidence that can sustain your spirit through the worst of times.

Delivered from Outside vs. Drawn from Inside

Those who seek relief rather than peace run into another major problem. They have no inward source from which to get relief but instead have to seek it from the outside, from sources beyond themselves. Whether they look for relief from athletics or alcohol, from sex or achievement, the relief they seek has to come from outside. So what happens when the body wears out, the booze dries up, the partner leaves, or the project fails?

"Aha!" someone might say. "All along you've been saying that we need to look to God for peace—but *he's* outside of us."

Well, yes and no.

Without question, God is beyond us and above us. As Paul said, God is "the blessed and only almighty God, the King of kings and Lord of lords. He alone can never die, and he lives in light so brilliant that no human can approach him. No one has ever seen him, nor ever will" (1 Tim. 6:15–16). God "himself gives life and breath to everything, and he satisfies every need there is" (Acts 17:25). So yes, he certainly is outside of us.

On the other hand, one of the greatest mysteries and blessings of the Christian faith is that God himself has chosen to live *within* his people, inside their very bodies. "Or don't you know that your body is the temple of the Holy Spirit, who lives in you and was given to you by God?" asks Paul (1 Cor. 6:19).

Since God is the God of peace (Rom. 15:33; 1 Cor. 14:33; Phil. 4:9), that means God's peace dwells within us and does not need to be supplied from the outside. Wherever a Christian

What do you do to seek out genuine peace as opposed to mere stress relief?

When life gets stressful, people ask God "Why?" That's nothing new. In the Bible Rebekah, Moses, Job, and even David did it. God's response? "You of little faith, why are you so afraid?" (Matt. 8:26 NIV). Peace is not the result of having a stress-free life. It's the result of trusting God in the midst of stress.

Ann-Margret Hovsepian, author

goes, God's peace tags along. This is why Jesus could say, "If you believe in me, come and drink! For the Scriptures declare that rivers of living water will flow out from within" (John 7:38). John explained that, "When he said 'living water,' he was speaking of the Spirit, who would be given to everyone believing in him" (v. 39).

The moment someone invites Jesus into his or her heart, the Holy Spirit takes up residence in that individual's body. From that moment on and for all eternity, the peace of God is available from *within*.

Despite that, we often try to find peace (or at least relief) from the outside. Sometimes we try to get relief from the pain of living not by downing some chemical substitute but by trying to outdo the other guy. But it doesn't work. If we really do leave our peers in our dust, satisfaction and peace still escape us. And if others remain "above" us, we get depressed.

Somebody will always be better than us in some area of life, often exactly where we want the top spot. Somebody will always rise above us in looks, or height, or education, or talent, or expertise—and that can devastate us if we feel the need to be number one. Even those in the top spots can have everything they need and still lack peace.

A lack of peace often results in anger at the world: anger at more successful people; anger at the past. Such angry individuals are forever talking about their bad luck and mistreatment, real or imagined. Some lose their peace for the rest of their lives. No one wants to be around them.

To experience God's peace, we must adopt God's goals, not the sick goals that end up destroying us. Human life lasts only seventy, maybe eighty years, and most people (especially in the West) have everything it takes to enjoy life. And yet how many peaceful people do you know?

The current chairman of our board, businessman Dave Hall, knows that chasing unworthy goals can rob a man of peace. He retired as a millionaire before he was fifty and today owns part of the NBA's Phoenix Suns. He's always been super competitive. After graduating from college, Dave took a job as a salesman with IBM; in his first year, the company named him top rookie salesman in the West. His second year he did even better, and his third year he won a big promotion.

"I was able to achieve virtually everything I wanted to achieve," Dave said. "I had a Porsche, a Jaguar, I had little animals all over my shirts. I had Maytag, KitchenAid. Everything I was working for that I thought was going to make me happy, I had, and I had very early. But it didn't give me what I thought it was going to give me."

At that stage of his life, Dave put his priorities in the following order: job success; happiness (which included his job success, money, and how much fun he was having); his children; and his wife and marriage. He thought, after all, *What could be a greater gift to my wife than for me to be successful?*

One day Dave's wife announced she thought they should start taking their family to church. It sounded like a good idea to Dave; wasn't that what every all-American family did? Besides, he'd probably make a lot of good business connections there.

At church Dave eventually found the peace he'd been missing. Life suddenly started to "click" for him with Jesus Christ in the driver's seat.

"It used to be that I worked to please only myself," he admitted. "But after that day when I committed my life to Christ, very shortly my priorities changed. They became: to love and serve God; my wife and my marriage; my children (and now my grandchildren); and my job and my business and financial success. And I'll say this: My business and financial success has been ten times greater as my fourth priority than as my first priority. When I wasn't paying as much attention to my business and financial success but was paying attention to my relationship with God, the Father who created me and knows me better than I know myself, my life changed immeasurably."

How would you describe the kind of peace God brings to your life?

Peace isn't the absence of problems. It's the serenity that settles in my heart when I believe that God is sheltering me, walking with me, and looking out for me. Philippians 4:7 is right in describing it as the peace that "transcends all understanding."

Ann-Margret Hovsepian, author

Dave discovered that true peace comes not from outside—not from competing and winning against the best—but from inside, as the Holy Spirit took up residence in his heart. And that's a lasting kind of peace that can survive even the worst drought.

Requires Increasing Dosages vs. Enjoys Growing Calm

When we seek relief from emotional pain through drugs or alcohol or self-destructive activity, we discover that our bodies quickly adjust, demanding ever-increasing amounts to maintain the same level of relief. What worked a year ago to bring some relief now has no effect at all.

God's peace works in an exactly opposite way. The more we allow his peace to calm our hearts, the steadier and calmer our lives become. What used to upset us a year ago now barely causes a ripple. The more his peace infuses our day-to-day lives, the more confident and assured and balanced we feel. And everyone notices.

The Quigley family can testify to this wonderful turn of events. Dawn Quigley and her three brothers grew up in a broken and dysfunctional family; none of them knew the Lord, and all of them had a fairly rough life. After Dawn placed her faith in Christ, she began praying for her three brothers. She felt overjoyed when the first of them gave his life to Christ and joined her in praying for their still-wild brothers. Eventually Darren, who had fought a hard battle with drugs and had spent time in jail, came to faith. That meant that only one brother, Dan, was left—but they knew he'd be the toughest. He was "about as far from God as possible," in his own words. He drank too much—often ordering his young daughter to bring him a drink—and liked to smoke marijuana. He thought "religion" was only for the weak and old ladies.

One day Darren asked Dan to come with him to a Palau crusade. Dan eventually agreed just to shut his brother up. Almost to show his contempt for the event, Dan smoked a joint and a half before the meeting. But despite the insult, the Lord spoke to his heart that day, and he too came to Jesus. Almost immediately God began cleaning up his life, and no one noticed more than the daughter he used to send for his drinks. "I grew up with him for eleven years, and I was really sad," she said. "But now our home is happy." Dan puts it like this: "I feel lighter."

Still, we shouldn't think God's peace magically appears in our lives. Certainly many young men and women have told me how God instantly lavished on them a deep feeling of peace the moment they trusted Jesus Christ for salvation. Even in their lives, however, God continues to build his peace gradually, over time. One of the most important ways he does this is through the fourth commandment:

Remember to observe the Sabbath day by keeping it holy. Six days a week are set apart for your daily duties and regular work, but the seventh day is a day of rest dedicated to the LORD your God. . . . For in six days the LORD made the heavens, the earth, the sea, and everything in them; then he rested on the seventh day. That is why the LORD blessed the Sabbath day and set it apart as holy.

Exodus 20:8–11

God created the Sabbath day for our benefit, to make us happy, joyful, and rested, but through the centuries we have managed to make it a strict, religious day. What a tragedy! The Lord tells us, "Work for six days, but give me this one day of rest. Use it to be happy and free and relaxed. Enjoy it, have some laughs, be with your family, and spend time with me in worship."

It makes all kinds of sense, doesn't it? For six days you work hard. You feel tense. You put everything you have into your schoolwork and your job, if you have one. But one day out of seven you give to the Lord. That day you are to rest from labor. Do you do that? If not, is it any wonder that you lack God's peace?

Of course, rest doesn't mean only that you lie on the beach. Rest also brings a confidence that God controls your life. When you keep God as your main priority, you enjoy a quiet rest and confidence that the Bible calls peace. "My gift of the Sabbath is inner rest," God says. "Rest of spirit. Rest of mind. Rest of conscience."

When I first came to the States, I didn't understand this inner rest that comes from knowing that the Lord Jesus lives inside every believer. Oh, I often heard about the "indwelling Lord Jesus." I "got it" intellectually. I understood the point. I even preached to others that Jesus Christ lives in us, that all his resources are available to us, that his resurrection life is our life, and that we live because he lives.

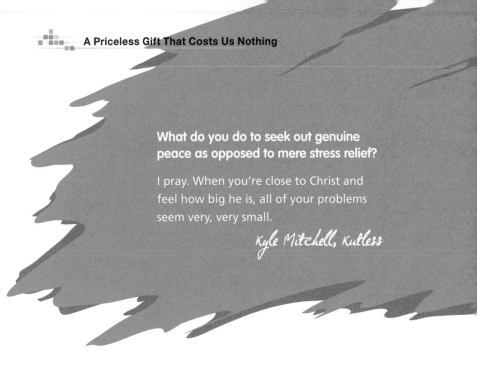

What do you do to seek out genuine peace as opposed to mere stress relief?

I pray. When you're close to Christ and feel how big he is, all of your problems seem very, very small.

Kyle Mitchell, Kutless

And yet, for some time I never rested in the finished work of Jesus Christ—and that produced in me a restlessness and a confusion and a continual nervousness.

Then one day I heard Major Ian Thomas speak in chapel at Multnomah Bible College (then called Multnomah School of the Bible). In a talk on Moses and the burning bush, this English gentleman turned the key that opened my spiritual understanding. "It's not your education that counts," he said. "It's not your connections that count. It's not your privileges that count. Any old bush will do, so long as God is in the bush." Then he quoted Galatians 2:20: "I am crucified with Christ."

And suddenly it all came together for me.

I ran to my bedroom and skipped my other classes. I fell on my knees and said, "O God, at last I get it. It's not I, but Christ living in me. The life I now live in the flesh, I live by faith in the Son of God, who loved me and gave himself for me."

I stayed on my knees for nearly two hours. I had been trying for seven or eight frustrating years to serve God in my own power, in my own knowledge, experience, and education. I thought I was sharp. But the Lord had shown me, "Luis, as long as you trust yourself, I can't use you. But if you will rely on the indwelling Christ—if you let Christ live in you and through you, if you start to see that it's not what you do for God but what God does in you and through you—then, Luis, I can use you."

It was a revolutionary thought, a revolutionary time. I was twenty-five years old and felt as though I had just been converted all over again. Finally I realized that the secret is not what we do for God but what God does in us and through us.

Soon I started preaching the same basic messages I had given before—but this time, to my surprise, people were converted. I saw a new power in the messages. I began to enjoy a freedom and a joy that I had never experienced. It suddenly felt exciting to serve the Lord; it was no longer a burden.

The Lord says to us, "Enter my rest and enjoy my peace." Have you entered that rest? Do you have peace in your heart? If Jesus Christ lives in you, you can and you should.

Expensive vs. Priceless

The expenses really pile up when you depend on chemical substitutes and human techniques to grab a little relief from the pain of life. On the other hand, God's peace costs us nothing—and yet no one can set a value on its worth.

Two businessmen came to some meetings we held in Australia. Both felt under terrible pressure. Both suffered tremendous business problems. Neither got along with their wives, and both felt the burden of nasty family troubles. When I gave the invitation to receive Jesus Christ, one of the businessmen opened his heart to the Lord. The other businessman became extremely angry and left the meeting, stomping all the way.

Three years later I returned to that city and inquired about these two men. The first settled affairs with his wife, and began to repay his debts and repair his business. Friends told me he learned to really love and obey God—and had a joyful family to prove it. This man finally discovered the peace of God.

The news about the second man broke my heart. A few weeks after our meetings, he climbed outside a tall building and jumped to his death. This man never discovered the peace of God.

The Bible says you can find peace with God through faith in our Lord Jesus Christ (Rom. 5:1). But to experience this peace you must open your life to Jesus Christ and receive him into your heart. It's a priceless gift that costs you nothing.

Yet it's also a gift we can refuse, even as believers. Colossians 3:15 says, "Let the peace that comes from Christ rule in your hearts." Did you notice the first word? "Let." God does not force his peace on anyone, not even his own children. We can have the peace of God . . . if we want it. We can allow his peace to rule in our lives and make us into a sweet aroma to those around us. But we must choose it.

Promoting the Prince of Peace

A few years ago the New Zealand *Herald* published an article on me under the headline "Promoting the Prince of Peace." I couldn't have said it better myself. I love to promote the Prince of Peace.

Some time ago I was in upstate New York for a week of prayer with several Presbyterian churches. An older gentleman approached me just before the service, limping and walking slowly with a cane.

"Young man," he said—he couldn't pronounce my name— "can I talk to you before you leave the area?"

"Yes," I said, and we set a time.

After the service I rode home with my host. "Luis," he said, "that was Dr. Smith. He's the most famous ophthalmologist on the East Coast. He's always been in the church, but he's never been happy. Now he wants to talk to you? This is marvelous."

On the day of our meeting, we all sat down and began to chat. After a cup of tea, he asked my hosts to leave the room.

"Young man," he said gravely, "I've got to ask you a question. When I was at university, John R. Mott, the well-known missionary, came to our school and challenged medical students to go and help the poor in certain parts of the world—in the Middle East and in Afghanistan. I felt the Lord sending me out, as well as my brother. But when I told my family and my fiancée, they all made fun of me. When I graduated from university, I turned down the Lord's call and married my sweetheart—we've been married now for forty years.

"But you know something, young man? I've now retired, I've made my little money, I've written my books—but for forty-two years I've never had a day of peace in my life. Now I'm an old man and on my way out, because my illness is serious.

"I want to go with my wife to Afghanistan to try to help the many people with poor vision. But my wife refuses to go. And now I want to ask you a question, and I'm going to act on your word: Shall I go, or shall I not go?"

Oh, boy, I thought, *what a decision for me to make.* I felt an impulse that I hoped came from the Lord, so I put my arms around this gentleman and said, "Doctor, you go."

He clung to me and began to weep.

"O Lord," he cried, "I'm going! I'm going and no one will stop me."

Then he prayed a prayer and left. And that was it.

Six months later I called up my former hosts and said, "How are you doing? And how is Doctor Smith?"

"Haven't you heard?" my friend asked. "He's in Afghanistan with his wife. He's like a teenager all over again! He is so excited. He returned to the States once already to visit the big pharmaceutical companies, pick up tons of medicine, and take it all back to Afghanistan. He's working for a while with a missionary, and he says he's never been so happy. But his body's falling apart."

The following Easter I visited New York for a week of evangelism. There was the doctor, his body a wreck. He could hardly talk by now, but he came to a luncheon we put together. "Luis," he whispered to me, "thank you for making me go to Afghanistan. I redeemed all the lost forty-two years *in just one year*! I'll never see you again except in the presence of the King, and I'll see you there."

About two months later the faithful physician went to be with the Lord.

Have you ever heard the call of God, like this doctor? Maybe the Lord spoke to you about going someplace or doing something. But you didn't respond—and you haven't enjoyed a day of peace since that moment. If that's you, then listen: It's never too late to plunge back into the stream of God's will for your life. Never!

If the Master has spoken to your heart, don't let another week go by without answering. And if the Lord is speaking to your heart right now, say, "Yes, Lord," because you will never have a day of peace if you remain outside of God's will. If you've been running away from the Lord, come back to him immediately and say, "I'm going, I'm going, and no one will stop me!"

HOW TO FIND Peace
ACCORDING TO THE BIBLE

1. **Recognize that peace eludes everyone who remains estranged from God.**

   "'There is no peace for the wicked,' says the LORD" (Isa. 48:22).

2. **Believe that God wants to give you his peace.**

   "May the Lord of peace himself always give you his peace no matter what happens" (2 Thess. 3:16).

3. **Accept that the way to peace is found by trusting in God.**

   "You will keep in perfect peace all who trust in you, whose thoughts are fixed on you!" (Isa. 26:3).

4. **Find peace with God through faith in Jesus Christ.**

   "Therefore, since we have been made right in God's sight by faith, we have peace with God because of what Jesus Christ our Lord has done for us" (Rom. 5:1).

5. **Realize that the peace of Jesus must be consciously accepted.**

   "I am leaving you with a gift—peace of mind and heart. And the peace I give isn't like the peace the world gives. So don't be troubled or afraid" (John 14:27).

6. **Look for peace in Jesus, not within yourself.**

   "I have told you all this so that you may have peace in me. Here on earth you will have many trials and sorrows. But take heart, because I have overcome the world" (John 16:33).

7. **Listen to what God says in his Word and turn away from foolishness.**

   "I listen carefully to what God the Lord is saying, for he speaks peace to his people, his faithful ones. But let them not return to their foolish ways" (Ps. 85:8).

8. **Make sure the Spirit of God guides your mind.**

   "If your sinful nature controls your mind, there is death. But if the Holy Spirit controls your mind, there is life and peace" (Rom. 8:6).

9. **Make it a habit to bring your concerns to God in prayer.**

   "Don't worry about anything; instead, pray about everything. Tell God what you need, and thank him for all he has done. If you do this, you will experience God's peace, which is far more wonderful than the human mind can understand. His peace will guard your hearts and minds as you live in Christ Jesus" (Phil. 4:6–7).

10. **Deliberately choose to become a peacemaker yourself.**

    "But the wisdom that comes from heaven is first of all pure. It is also peace loving, gentle at all times, and willing to yield to others. It is full of mercy and good deeds. It shows no partiality and is always sincere. And those who are peacemakers will plant seeds of peace and reap a harvest of goodness" (James 3:17–18).

WISE WORDS

IF YOU FORGIVE THOSE WHO SIN AGAINST YOU, YOUR HEAVENLY FATHER WILL FORGIVE YOU. BUT IF YOU REFUSE TO FORGIVE OTHERS, YOUR FATHER WILL NOT FORGIVE YOUR SINS.

jesus,
Matthew 6:14

A Fresh Start

Acceptance or Forgiveness?

Behind what used to be called "The Iron Curtain," millions grew up in an atheistic, completely secular society. Citizens of the former Soviet Union and other European Communist countries heard nothing about Christ, faith, or forgiveness. Their teachers scoffed at the church and assured the people that only weak-minded old women bothered with such superstitions. And yet powerful feelings of guilt continued to hound the people.

While visiting the former Soviet Union a few years ago, I heard about a Russian pastor who was busy supervising a rebuilding project aimed at converting a ruined building into a home for a Baptist church. One day a man walked in and asked, "Is the priest here?" Russians have no word for pastor; they use the term *priest* for clergymen of all denominations.

"I am the priest," the pastor replied.

"There are four young women out there who want to talk to you," the man said.

"Please tell them to come in."

"They don't want to come in. They refuse to come in."

So the pastor walked outside, where he found four pretty young women, perhaps no older than eighteen, nervously waiting for him. When he extended his hand in greeting, they simultaneously dropped their heads and refused even to touch him.

"We are not worthy to shake your hands," they said.

"Why aren't you worthy to shake my hand?"

"We are all prostitutes," one answered. "The reason we've come to talk to you is that we wanted to know—will God ever forgive us for what we've done?"

The pastor pulled out his Bible and said, "Of course he'll forgive you." Then he told them about the death of Christ and the blood that cleanses from all guilt.

"But would God ever forgive us?" they asked again, desperately. "We've done such awful things!"

"He'll forgive you right now if you invite him into your heart."

Without hesitation all four declared, "We want to invite him into our hearts."

And so right there, on the sidewalk for everyone to see, this pastor led four troubled young women to faith in Jesus Christ. When they finished praying, they raised their heads and through tears asked the pastor, "Are we forgiven now?"

"Yes, you are forgiven," he replied. "The blood of Jesus cleanses from all sin. So you are forgiven."

With that assurance, the four leaped into the air, hugged each other, and exclaimed, "We are forgiven! We are forgiven!" Then they turned to the pastor and gave him a big hug. "*Now* we can come into the church," they said firmly.

 words or less

When our actions injure or damage a cherished relationship, we need more than mere acceptance. "Excuse me" can never fully substitute for "Forgive me."

And so all five entered the ruined building and sat down amid the rubble, and this faithful pastor explained the way of salvation more clearly.

I'm So Unworthy

You can't imagine how many individuals all over the world have told me, "I feel exactly like those young women. I have committed so many sins. I am so unworthy."

While the Bible insists that Jesus Christ offers forgiveness as a free gift, many of us think, *I've got to become religious first. I have to pay my dues. I have to get my act together.*

None of that is true. The Bible says God longs to set you free if you open your heart to Jesus Christ and say, "Lord Jesus, I am unworthy. You know what I've thought and done. But if you really died for me, Lord, and you rose from the dead—then please cleanse my conscience. Forgive my past. Set me free!"

Every one of us, if we're honest, knows that we need forgiveness. Yet many times we don't seek out what we really need. We settle for acceptance when we really need forgiveness.

The difference isn't as subtle as it might first appear. Forgiveness wipes the slate clean, while acceptance merely covers it. The first says, "Forgive me"; the second says, "Excuse me." Forgiveness fully acknowledges the wrong that has been done, while acceptance often minimizes the offense just to keep the relationship going. Yet to feel like fully whole people, what we really need is forgiveness, a wiping clean of the slate.

Forgiveness outperforms mere acceptance in at least five important ways:

Acceptance	Forgiveness
• Offers a way to continue	• Permits a fresh start
• Supplies an emotional breather	• Provides emotional release
• Based on technique	• Based on truth
• Manages guilt	• Removes guilt
• Stops the bleeding	• Fosters healing

We ought to accept others for who and what they are, but when our actions injure or damage a cherished relationship, we need more than mere acceptance. "Excuse me" can never fully substitute for "Forgive me."

Offers a Way to Continue vs. Permits a Fresh Start

We like to hear a friend say, "Just forget about it," when we pull some boneheaded move. And very often nothing more is necessary. Friends accept other friends and understand that everybody makes mistakes. "Just forget about it," "It's okay," and "Let's just move on" work fine much of the time. An attitude of acceptance allows us to continue, to keep plowing ahead.

Sometimes, however, we don't need a way to continue so much as we require a fresh start. Some patterns need to be broken—but they'll never come to an end if we don't stop dead in our tracks, name them for what they are, express genuine sorrow for the pain we have caused, and ask for forgiveness.

Did you know that *repentance* is the most positive word in the English language? I never thought of it like that until I heard my friend John Hunter make the claim. We usually think of *repentance* as a sad, dark, and horrible term; actually, it's the beginning of a new life. It's leaving the past behind. It's starting over. *Repentance* is a very liberating word.

To repent means simply to admit the truth and to start moving in a different direction. Repentance doesn't mean groveling in the dirt and acting weird. Repentance is a deep conviction that I did wrong, I hurt other people, I offended God—and I want to change. That's really the only way to start over. Repentance means taking responsibility for our actions and saying, "Yes, I've sinned against my friend or my classmate, I am sorry for it, and by the power of God I intend to start behaving in a healthier way."

Many years ago I heard a sermon on forgiving others as Jesus Christ forgave us (Col. 3:13). The speaker explained how a father can alienate his children by something he did years before. "Maybe it's as small as a broken promise," he said.

That sermon burned a hole into my soul. I returned home quickly and separately called in my twin sons, who were then about nine years old.

"Kevin," I said to the first, "have I ever promised you anything that I haven't fulfilled? Or have I ever said anything to you that hurt your feelings but never asked you for forgiveness?"

"Yes, Dad," he immediately replied. "Last Christmas you promised Keith and me a special toy that I really wanted and you never gave it to me."

I hugged my son and said, "Kevin, please forgive me."

"I forgive you, Dad."

"Okay, Kevin, we're going to the shopping center today and I'm going to buy you that toy. Anything else I promised you but never delivered?"

"No, I can't remember anything."

I dismissed Kevin and called in Keith. "Keith," I said, "have I ever really hurt your feelings but never asked you for forgiveness?"

"Yes."

I didn't expect *that* answer.

"What did I do?" I asked.

"Do you remember when Stephen was born?"

He had appeared on the scene six years earlier.

"Yes, I remember. What happened?"

"Do you remember when Mom was going to have Stephen, you jumped in the car and took off for the hospital?"

"Yes, I remember that."

"You came back a half hour later. You had forgotten the suitcase for the baby."

"I don't remember that."

"Well, I remember."

"And what happened?"

"The suitcase was all messed up and you spanked me because you thought I had messed it up."

"But you didn't mess it up?"

"No. One of the neighbor boys did it."

Boy, I felt so rotten. Six years! Keith had never forgotten that I spanked him unjustly. I immediately drew him close and said, "Keith, I spanked you for something you didn't do. Will you forgive me?"

"Sure, I forgive you."

Acceptance provides a good and necessary service, but it will never heal the wounds that only repentance and forgiveness can treat. Sometimes we hurt someone and quickly forget the incident—but the injured party never does. Multiply forgotten toys and undeserved spankings by a thousand, and you soon begin to see the necessary place of repentance and forgiveness.

Offers an Emotional Breather vs. Provides Emotional Release

When we have done something wrong to a person, acceptance allows the relationship to continue by providing an emotional breather from the pain.

But unless we forgive—until we bring the problem into the light and fully and finally deal with it—we're only shooting Novocain into an infected foot. The treatment brings some relief from the pain and allows us to continue walking, but the infection never gets any better.

An emotional breather feels nice, but emotional freedom feels a whole lot better. Parole may brighten our day, but freedom brightens our life. And freedom really is the issue.

In Matthew 18 Jesus told a parable about the necessity of forgiving others. Those who refuse to forgive, he said, would only slam the door on their own jail cell. Unforgiving people can expect only "anger" and "prison," Jesus said. And he ended his story with the sobering words, "That's what my heavenly

Father will do to you if you refuse to forgive your brothers and sisters in your heart" (verse 35).

Jesus doesn't want that for us. He wants us to walk free! A young Scottish woman made this discovery after spending several years behind emotional bars. Her father abandoned the family and took off to work in Saudi Arabia. Bitterness gripped her heart, and over time a nasty grudge against her father grew steadily larger. Eventually she gave her life to Jesus Christ, but still she refused to forgive her dad.

One day she heard the words of Jesus: "If you forgive those who sin against you, your heavenly Father will forgive you. But if you refuse to forgive others, your Father will not forgive your sins" (Matt. 6:14–15). She took her Lord's warning to heart and wrote a letter to her father, telling him that because of Jesus's love, she forgave him for walking away and never returning.

To her surprise, the heartbroken old man immediately wrote a reply asking for her forgiveness—and asking her mother if he could come home.

Forgiveness sets you free. If you allow yourself to grow bitter and angry in your heart, you are the one who pays.

Bible teacher Bill Gothard used to tell a story about a teenager who held a bitter grudge against a relative. When a youth worker suggested that she should forgive that relative, the girl said, "I'll never forgive that person as long as I live."

"I'm sorry to hear that," replied the youth worker.

"Why?" asked the girl.

"Because in twenty years, you will be just like that relative," came the answer. This thought so horrified the girl that she quickly said, "Oh, no! In that case I'll forgive her right now."

We are free when we forgive!

Based on Technique vs. Based on Truth

While we all recognize our need for forgiveness, we have developed lots of ways to deal with guilt apart from forgiveness.

Would you rather be accepted by God or forgiven by him?

To be accepted by God would mean that he accepted exactly who I am right now, with all of my sins. Instead, I would rather be forgiven. When God forgives, he washes away the past and writes a fresh future for us, all the time still accepting us where we are today.

Elizabeth Honeycutt,
contributing author,
Starting Point Study Bible

We deny it. We try to dull its pain through drugs or alcohol. We try to ignore it, pacify it, redefine it. We become atheists, hoping that our feelings of guilt will go away if we make God go away. We try to make up for our evil deeds with good deeds. And some who grow tired of the struggle commit suicide. But none of these techniques ultimately work, because they never deal completely with the truth of our guilt. You cannot do enough penance to remove your guilt. Only Jesus Christ has the power and wisdom to get rid of it at its source. As the apostle Paul said, "You were dead because of your sins and because your sinful nature was not yet cut away. Then God made you alive with Christ. He forgave all our sins. He canceled the record that contained the charges against us. He took it and destroyed it by nailing it to Christ's cross" (Col. 2:13–14).

Several years ago during an encounter with the Communist Party secretary of Ecuador, I had only the truth of Jesus Christ to offer.

This woman, a bitter revolutionary, came to see me after watching one of our call-in television programs. She cursed me out, insulted me repeatedly, and proudly described herself as an atheist. She said she came from an upper-class, Catholic background but long ago had abandoned the church. When her mother died, she attended the funeral primarily to mock the archbishop, who did the honors. She had married and divorced three times and seethed with anger. But I could tell she felt profoundly guilty for her revolutionary activities.

So I thought, *What Bible verse shall I quote?* Hebrews 10:17— and *only* Hebrews 10:17—came to mind: "Your sins and lawless acts I will remember no more."

"Well, I don't believe the Bible is the Word of God," she spat at me.

"You may not believe it," I said, "but God says, 'Your sins and lawless acts I will remember no more.'"

"Oh, you priests are all alike! Cheats and liars every one."

"Even if that were true," I repeated, "God still says, 'Your sins and lawless acts I will remember no more.'"

Our wrestling match went on for an hour and a half. I counted how many times I quoted the verse: seventeen. Toward the end she began to cry. "If there is a God," she said, "do you think he would forgive a woman like me?"

And I repeated one last time, "Your sins and lawless acts I will remember no more."

She paused, then said slowly, "If God can forgive me, he can forgive anyone in the world." And right there she asked the Lord Jesus to forgive her sins and make her clean.

How does Christ forgive us? First, he forgives us while we are still guilty: "But God showed his great love for us by sending Christ to die for us while we were still sinners" (Rom. 5:8). Christ died on the cross to forgive us when we were still rebels. All he asks is that we come to him with sincere hearts and say, "God, please forgive me and make me your child." As the apostle Paul said, "For if you confess with your mouth that Jesus is Lord and believe in your heart that God raised him from the dead, you will be saved" (Rom. 10:9).

Jesus deals with our guilt not by applying some sophisticated technique but by taking our sin upon himself. How? "God made Christ, who never sinned, to be the offering for our sin, so that we could be made right with God through Christ" (2 Cor. 5:21).

The moments right before I stand to preach the gospel to a crowd of thousands—whether I'm in Los Angeles, London, Hong Kong, or Guatemala City—hold a mixture of emotions.

I feel thankfulness to God for granting me another harvest time opportunity. I feel anticipation and joy knowing that God is patiently at work in many hearts.

And until recently I felt sadness because the thoughts of this father would almost always turn to Andrew.

Andrew is my third of four sons. After graduating from the University of Oregon, Andrew moved to Boston, where as a confident young man he began his climb up the corporate ladder. But it wasn't his distance from home that troubled my heart; it was his distance from the Lord.

Like our other sons, Andrew had prayed to invite Jesus to come into his heart when he was a child. Since high school, however, he had shown little interest in the Bible and church. "Fraternity life" ruled in college. God occasionally stepped in but could not fit in. Andrew lived a secular lifestyle with secular values.

Painful as it was, Pat and I had to accept what we had counseled other parents. Just because Andrew grew up with Sunday school, memorized Scripture verses, was baptized, and even respected and defended the gospel did not mean he was truly converted. Conversion is essential for everyone, whether born into a pagan family or a totally absorbing Christian family. Andrew's life denied a personal conversion experience.

And so often, as I sat on the platform and prayed, "Lord, may many come forward to confess Christ," I'd be thinking, *There's no greater joy than this . . . but what about Andrew? How can my joy be complete until Andrew walks with Christ?*

I realized that if my heart carried this weight, God's heart must feel even sadder, because his love is so much more selfless and pure.

Then one day Andrew returned to the Lord. Pat and I took him with us to Jamaica for a crusade. There he met Robert Levy, the crusade's finance chairman, his son Chris, and his daughter Wendy. Their energetic commitment to Christ convicted Andrew of his wild ways. Though his good intentions to change subsequently failed, weeks later another visit to Jamaica (to see Wendy) led to what Andrew calls "some serious repenting."

Was it first-time repentance and genuine belief? Was it a recommitment to Christ? To me it doesn't matter. I just rejoice that the Spirit of God is living in him. Andrew is born of God and is acting like a child of God should.

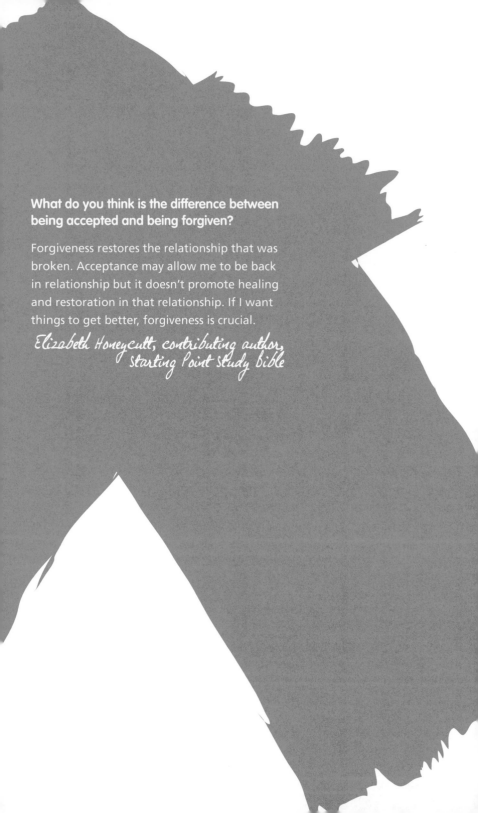

What do you think is the difference between being accepted and being forgiven?

Forgiveness restores the relationship that was broken. Acceptance may allow me to be back in relationship but it doesn't promote healing and restoration in that relationship. If I want things to get better, forgiveness is crucial.

Elizabeth Honeycutt, contributing author, Starting Point Study Bible

I now preach the gospel with even more conviction. The resurrected Christ has the power to change America, where 80 percent of the people claim to be Christians but few live any differently from pagans or atheists. Their hearts have not been changed, and unless Jesus Christ changes their hearts, they never will be any different from those outside the Christian faith.

To me, Andrew is a beautiful picture of what I'd like to see God do for your generation in America. Because when the Lord Jesus forgives, he forgives *completely*.

Manages Guilt vs. Removes Guilt

Most psychologists will tell you that unresolved guilt accounts for about 80 percent of all psychological and psychiatric problems. People desperately want relief from guilt.

Even the best among us have skeletons in our closet, secrets known to no one else. Maybe you slept with a boyfriend or girlfriend. Maybe you cheated on a major test. Maybe you lied about some incident or event. You're smart enough to cover it up, but inside you feel rotten and guilty.

The question is, how can we best deal with guilt? What should we *do* with it? A lot of young people today try to *manage* their personal guilt—keep it under control, under wraps. They've tried and failed to deny it; they can't see how to rid themselves of it; so they learn little tricks to keep the guilt inside.

They're right about one thing: Guilt *is* real. We all grapple with guilt. But Jesus Christ wants to do more than *manage* guilt; Jesus wants to *remove* it:

> Jesus climbed into a boat and went back across the lake to his own town. Some people brought to him a paralyzed man on a mat. Seeing their faith, Jesus said to the paralyzed man, "Take heart, son! Your sins are forgiven."
>
> "Blasphemy! This man talks like he is God!" some of the teachers of religious law said among themselves.

> Jesus knew what they were thinking, so he asked them, "Why are you thinking such evil thoughts? Is it easier to say, 'Your sins are forgiven' or 'Get up and walk'? I will prove that I, the Son of Man, have the authority on earth to forgive sins." Then Jesus turned to the paralyzed man and said, "Stand up, take your mat, and go on home, because you are healed!"
>
> And the man jumped up and went home!

Matthew 9:1–7

We all wrestle with guilt, but left to ourselves, we remain down on the mat. Jesus gives us a way to *get rid of it* altogether. The Bible says guilt can be wiped out from our conscience through faith in Jesus Christ. When we come to him in faith, Jesus Christ will "purify our hearts from deeds that lead to death so that we can worship the living God" (Heb. 9:14). We can try to manage our guilt, but only Jesus can remove our guilt and cleanse our conscience, something far beyond the ability of even the most gifted psychiatrist or psychologist. They can help by pinpointing problems, but none would dare to say, "I can remove your guilt." Jesus does say it.

Of course, not everyone celebrates Jesus's work. Some complain that accepting Jesus's offer of forgiveness is an easy way out—too easy.

It may be "easy" for us to rid ourselves of guilt, but it wasn't easy at all for Christ. To make our forgiveness possible he had to give up for a while the glories of heaven, take on a human body, suffer at the hands of brutal enemies, die on a Roman cross, and rise from the tomb on the third day. It was no "easy way out" for him! "He died for us," wrote the apostle Paul, "so that we can live with him forever" (1 Thess. 5:10).

And live without guilt!

Still, as I said, not everyone celebrates. A caller to a radio program I was on who identified himself as a member of the National Secular Society strenuously objected to my take on guilt and forgiveness.

"Religion says that suffering is out there and it's bad," he said, "but also says it has the explanation for it: you are guilty, you are the sinners, you have original sin inherited from Adam and Eve—who are, incidentally, fictional. All religion does is transfer the guilt for everything that goes wrong in the world onto human beings, which I think is a terrible thing to do. The priests have done this for their own purposes. I mean, if you can convince people that they're guilty, that they need Jesus or the church or whatever to save them, then you have control over them. A famous humanist once said that Christianity not only has the unique advantage of turning men and women into slaves, it also teaches them to love their chains—and this is what Luis Palau is doing here. He is teaching them to love their chains, to accept that they are guilty, and then spend their lives groveling in the dirt, saying how wonderful it is that they've been relieved of their guilt."

But this is all wrong. Jesus does not want us to grovel in the dirt; he wants to lift us from the dust (where we put ourselves) and help us to soar high into the skies. If my humanist friend were correct, then the only people struggling with guilt should be those with some connection to church—but I know from traveling the world that the phenomenon of guilt penetrates every culture, nation, community, and human heart.

In the past few years we've held a unique kind of outreach event called Beachfest in places like Fort Lauderdale, Florida, on the East Coast, and Santa Cruz, California, on the West Coast. Two sisters came to one Beachfest with a church's youth group; the younger sister willingly, the older sister only because her mother insisted.

Soon, though, both girls were having a great time. And when my friend and associate Ron Luce spoke on a Thursday night, they both gave their hearts and lives to Jesus. The following Sunday morning the church's youth worker spoke with the girls' mother. The mother was upset because she had found some letters and material in her older daughter's room that led her to

Why do you think we find it so hard to say "forgive me" rather than "excuse me"?

Frankly, we don't like to admit when we're wrong. "Excuse me" implies, "If you hadn't been in my way, I wouldn't have hurt you." Instead, "forgive me" says, "I realize that I have wronged you and I apologize." To ask forgiveness takes true humility.

Elizabeth Ries Jones,
author and editor

think she was experimenting with drugs. She had not yet seen her daughters, since they had been staying at a friend's house, and she just didn't know how to handle the situation. She felt as though she were losing her daughter; every time they spoke, the daughter seemed to be pushing the mother further away. When the woman's daughters came to church, the older one started crying in the sanctuary. She felt so overcome with guilt by what she had done that she couldn't wait to come clean with her mother. The mother and older daughter went home and talked for two and a half hours.

God has brought a great change to that household! And he did it through the power of forgiveness.

Don't settle for "managing" your guilt. And don't bother trying to deny it. Let Jesus Christ remove it, once and for all.

Stops the Bleeding vs. Fosters Healing

When we hurt someone or someone hurts us, acceptance can act as a kind of relational tourniquet. The decision to accept someone despite an offense stops the bleeding in a relationship and allows us to carry on.

Yet it's no final solution, because stopping the bleeding isn't the same as healing the wound. We use tourniquets for emergencies, not as a permanent solution. Once we get the bleeding stopped, we need to start the healing process—and in relationships, that occurs only through forgiveness.

If your world is hurting, breaking up, or suffering because of something you have done, what can you do? Let me tell you what the Bible says.

First, stop being so arrogant and humble yourself. Colossians 3:12 says, "Since God chose you to be the holy people whom he loves, you must clothe yourselves with tenderhearted mercy, kindness, humility, gentleness, and patience." Now, most of us don't want to humble ourselves. But if your relationships are hurting, or if they aren't what you want them to be, humbly admit your failure, your fault, or the hurt you've caused.

Second, we are to forgive one another. The very next verse in Colossians says, "You must make allowance for each other's faults and forgive the person who offends you. Remember, the Lord forgave you, so you must forgive others" (Col. 3:13).

One of the best ways to start over and mend your relationship problems is for you to forgive from the heart. It works!

Nationally syndicated newspaper columnist Dr. Robert Wallace gave exactly that advice to an eighteen-year-old who felt torn by tragic family circumstances.[1] The young man wrote:

> I'm 18 and live with my mother and older brother. My parents went through a very bitter divorce four years ago and because my brother and I were loyal to our mom, we severed all contact with Dad. The basic problem was our dad's drinking habit.
>
> Last week Dad's mother (our grandmother) called and said our father had a severe heart attack and she wanted my brother and me to go to the hospital to see him. She said he wanted to talk with us in case he was going to die. My brother said he wanted nothing whatsoever to do with our father and wouldn't even go to Dad's funeral if he died.
>
> I don't feel that way. Dad did some things I'm not proud of, but I have forgiven him in my heart. I'd like to visit my father, but I know both my brother and mom don't want me to see him even though they didn't come out and say as much.
>
> Should I see my dad and risk causing tension with the two people I love most on this earth, or feel guilty that I didn't have the courage to talk with him when something drastic could happen to him? I'm not quite sure I will heed your advice, but I would like to hear your thoughts on this.
>
> Nameless, Frederick, MD

Dr. Wallace wisely replied, "I can tell that you've made your decision, and it's the right one. You have forgiven your father. By all means, go see him. Don't allow your mother and brother to dissuade you from doing so. If you don't see him now, you may never see him again, and that will haunt you the rest of your life. Indeed, your courage in this matter may open up your brother's heart as well, or at least begin the process. Harboring a lifelong hatred of his dad, however justified, will only stunt his own life."

The road to healing doesn't always roll along smoothly, of course. Many times restitution—making things right—must accompany the forgiveness package. Those who have truly received the forgiveness of God naturally want to make things right, so far as they can, with those they've hurt. When Zacchaeus received the forgiveness of Jesus in Luke 19, he immediately turned around and said, "I will give half my wealth to the poor, Lord, and if I have overcharged people on their taxes, I will give them back four times as much!" (v. 8).

The message of Jesus Christ does not teach irresponsibility. We are to ask forgiveness from one another and, if necessary, make restitution to one another. If you cheated a friend or disrespected your mom or dad, then humble yourself and ask him or her to forgive you. Maybe it's too late to go back to square one, but the gospel pushes us to make things right, to whatever degree we can. "Do your part to live in peace with everyone," says the apostle Paul, "as much as possible" (Rom. 12:18).

Genuine forgiveness gives you peace wth God and helps you to reconcile with those you've wronged. Do you have the same assurance? You can, so long as you come to the same Lord for forgiveness.

HOW TO RECEIVE Forgiveness
ACCORDING TO THE BIBLE

1. **Realize that forgiveness flows from God's love, not your worthiness.**

   "Please pardon the sins of this people because of your magnificent, unfailing love, just as you have forgiven them ever since they left Egypt" (Num. 14:19).

2. **Recognize that God's mercy holds back his judgment.**

   "Yet he was merciful and forgave their sins and didn't destroy them all. Many a time he held back his anger and did not unleash his fury!" (Ps. 78:38).

3. **Understand that God wants to grant you forgiveness through Jesus Christ.**

   "For he has rescued us from the one who rules in the kingdom of darkness, and he has brought us into the Kingdom of his dear Son. God has purchased our freedom with his blood and has forgiven all our sins" (Col. 1:13–14).

4. **Confess your sins to God.**

   "But if we confess our sins to him, he is faithful and just to forgive us and to cleanse us from every wrong" (1 John 1:9).

5. **Turn away from your sins and determine to walk in a new direction.**

   "All must turn from their sins and turn to God—and prove they have changed by the good things they do" (Acts 26:20).

6. **Believe that Jesus died and rose again to give you forgiveness.**

   "Jesus is ordained of God to be the judge of all—the living and the dead. He is the one all the prophets testified about, saying that everyone who believes in him will have their sins forgiven through his name" (Acts 10:42–43).

7. **Declare your dependence upon Jesus.**

   "For if you confess with your mouth that Jesus is Lord and believe in your heart that God raised him from the dead, you will be saved" (Rom. 10:9).

8. **Once you receive forgiveness, practice forgiving others.**

   "You must make allowance for each other's faults and forgive the person who offends you. Remember, the Lord forgave you, so you must forgive others" (Col. 3:13).

9. **Don't "keep score" of the offenses committed against you.**

   "Then Peter came to him and asked, 'Lord, how often should I forgive someone who sins against me? Seven times?'

   "'No!' Jesus replied, 'seventy times seven!'" (Matt. 18:21–22).

10. **Don't allow resentment to derail your forgiveness.**

    "But when you are praying, first forgive anyone you are holding a grudge against, so that your Father in heaven will forgive your sins, too" (Mark 11:25).

WISE WORDS

REMEMBER THAT IN A RACE EVERYONE RUNS, BUT ONLY ONE PERSON GETS THE PRIZE. YOU ALSO MUST RUN IN SUCH A WAY THAT YOU WILL WIN. ALL ATHLETES PRACTICE STRICT SELF-CONTROL. THEY DO IT TO WIN A PRIZE THAT WILL FADE AWAY, BUT WE DO IT FOR AN ETERNAL PRIZE.

the apostle Paul,
1 Corinthians 9:24-25

A Sense
of Destiny

Activity or Significance?

It has to rank as one of the saddest television shows I've ever seen.

Two men had developed an unusual friendship. One had climbed the corporate ladder to become a wealthy and powerful executive. The other had never accomplished much of anything; despite a good mind and strong self-confidence, he ended up a bum. Yet the two men could talk about personal issues and confront each other with hard truths in ways that no one else could. They maintained their odd friendship even while screaming their lungs out at each other.

One day doctors told the executive he didn't have long to live; his heart could fail at any time. The man urgently needed a heart transplant, but he wasn't eligible for one. When the bum learned the news, he offered to donate his own heart to his friend—effectively sentencing himself to death. Horrified state officials refused to allow the procedure, so the bum filed a lawsuit to permit the operation to move ahead.

"I don't want to get to the end of my life and not have accomplished anything," he angrily explained. "I've done nothing of value! Now I can really do something with my life. So what if I live forty more years and *still* do nothing? But if I give my heart to this man, I will not have lived in vain."

By the end of the show the bum had lost his case, leaving me as a viewer with a feeling of deep sadness both for the dying man and for the living man who wanted to die.

Do you identify even a little with the man who wanted to give up his heart? Do you feel as if your life is going nowhere fast? If so, be encouraged. You *can* take steps to correct the problem.

Do I Count?

All of us need to feel that our lives count for something, that we exist for some purpose, that our existence has meaning. We all want a sense of destiny. And we need to feel significant. That is why so many of us ask the crucial questions:

Who am I?
Why am I here?
Where am I going?
Who put me on Earth and what does he want from me?
What's the purpose for my life?

I firmly believe that a purpose for your life *does* exist. There *is* a divine plan. And you can find the answers to your most significant questions when you meet Jesus Christ.

"But don't all religions give those answers?" some ask.

No, not at all. And anybody who claims this just hasn't been paying attention. I have often been in India among Hindus, in

China among Buddhists, in Japan among Shintoists. None of them pretends to tell you who you are, where you came from, or your purpose in life. No world religion other than Christianity tries to tell you what happens when you die or claims to give you the assurance of eternal life.

Each of us wants more than just a nice life, close friends, plenty of money, some fun, and good health. Deep inside we all seek spiritual purpose. Because God "has planted eternity in the human heart" (Eccles. 3:11), we will all feel unhappiness and frustration until we find and live out our God-given purpose.

Activity or Significance?

Our society doesn't seem particularly good at discovering purpose or meaning. It seems more proficient at activity—and the more energetic and nonstop, the better.

While all of us need to know that we matter, sometimes we settle for keeping really busy. We tell ourselves that if we're always busy, that must mean we're important. While inside we're dying for a sense of purpose and destiny, we settle for busyness.

Of course, I see nothing wrong with keeping a full schedule. The apostle Paul told the Corinthians, "We work hard with our own hands" (1 Cor. 4:12 NIV), and he encouraged them in turn to "be strong and steady, always enthusiastic about the Lord's work, for you know that nothing you do for the Lord is ever useless" (1 Cor. 15:58).

God himself praises useful activity, so long as it serves a worthwhile purpose. The problem is mistaking busyness for significance. Just because we're busy doesn't mean that we're fulfilling some grand purpose. The trick is to get busy about the right things.

Why does it pay to seek meaning before busyness? Let me suggest five areas of comparison.

God wants us to be busy about the right things.

25 words or less

Activity	Significance
• Efficient	• Effective
• Keeps busy	• Pursues meaning
• Seeks worth	• Enjoys worth
• Tyranny of the urgent	• Triumph of the important
• Gains admirers	• Attracts colleagues

God wants us to be busy with the right things.

Efficient vs. Effective

Some students treat efficiency as if it were the holy grail of education. They do everything they can to refine their study habits into the most efficient system possible. Yet many of them still fail. Why?

Because "efficient" doesn't necessarily mean "effective." You can efficiently study the wrong subject. Have you ever spent an "all nighter" studying a certain part of your notes for a big test the next day—and then discovered that most of the questions had to do with something else entirely?

A few years back I met someone in real life who, without even knowing it, chose efficiency over effectiveness. Someone invited me to give a brief Bible study for a small group that met every Tuesday for lunch. Of the six regular attenders, three followed Jesus Christ and three were searching.

I told a story about an English princess who wanted to find assurance of eternal life.

As I told the story, I saw tears trickling down the cheeks of one especially wealthy man. He tried to cover it up, but I noticed. And I thought, *Ahh . . . something is going on inside.* When the lunch ended, I walked over to him and said, "Jimmy, I noticed you were crying when I told the story of the princess."

"Yes," he admitted, a little startled, "you caught me."

"Why were you crying?" I asked.

In great frustration he blurted out, "Why is it that I've gone to church since I was a kid, but I still feel as if my life lacks purpose? I've never had the assurance of eternal life—and here I am, sixty-five! Why am I missing out?"

I gave a few brief answers, but soon he had to leave for his office at the insurance firm he owned. I asked him to meet me for lunch during the week.

So a few days later we met at a club downtown. As soon as we sat down, swarms of well-wishers came by the table to say, "Hi, Jimmy!" "How are you doing, Jimmy?" "How's your wife, Jimmy?" Money can win you a lot of friends but not necessarily a purpose in life.

When his cloud of admirers finally left us alone, Jimmy asked, "Why did you invite me to lunch?" He thought I would ask for money. But I had bigger things in mind.

"Jimmy," I replied, "the other day you told me that you didn't have the assurance of eternal life. Before lunch is over, I want you to go home with that assurance."

As his eyes turned red, he said, "I've got to tell you why I said that, Luis. I had a brother—we were partners in business—and he committed suicide just a year and a half ago. He didn't leave a note, he didn't leave a letter. He had not committed immorality, he was a good husband, he was successful in business, he had no debts. I cannot explain why my brother took his life."

He paused, then continued. "I have five kids, and all of them are unbelievers—basically, they say they're atheists. And I cannot figure it out. I've gone to church all my life. I took them with me when they were kids. But now they refuse to come to church, and none of them follow Jesus Christ today." He confessed that he'd failed his kids, failed his wife, failed as a spiritual person. And then he began to weep quietly at the table.

"Jimmy," I said, "don't go blaming yourself. Let's not talk about your kids. Let's think about that later. The most important thing right now is that you personally open your heart to Jesus Christ."

"My church is only three blocks away," he answered. "Why don't we go over there to pray?"

"Jimmy," I replied, "I want you to pray now, right here."

"Right *here*? At the lunch table?" he asked nervously. "But everybody in the club is watching me."

"So don't close your eyes," I said. "They will never know we are praying. Keep your eyes open."

And right there in that restaurant, this powerful business-man with the efficient insurance operation invited Jesus Christ into his life. For sixty-five years he had lived without a sense of purpose. He felt guilty because his kids had rebelled, confused because his brother took his life. All that began to change when he asked the Lord to come into his heart. Jimmy continues to meet with other Christian businessmen to pray and study the Bible together.

After a lifetime of business success but personal disappoint-ment, Jimmy has exchanged efficiency for effectiveness. You haven't lived nearly as long as Jimmy, but are you on the same track he was on? Are you *efficient* in school or in sports or some-where else but *ineffective* in life, in what really counts? How you answer can determine the quality of the rest of your life.

Keeps Busy vs. Pursues Meaning

A scene from the old science fiction movie *Starman* illustrates for me much of modern culture. In the film, an alien stranded on Earth takes on the appearance of a man who had just died. The man's widow befriends the alien and helps him reach a rendezvous point where his alien pals can pick him up. Along the way the pair endures a series of traumatic encounters.

In one scene, Starman has to drive a car, even though he's never before taken the wheel. He has watched his friend drive, however, so he thinks he knows what to do. As they approach a busy intersection, the signal turns yellow. He runs the light, nearly causing a terrible accident. His terrified companion chews

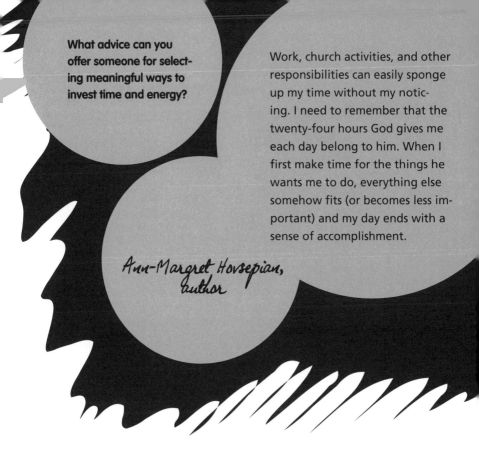

him out for almost getting them killed and asks if he really understands the rules of the road. Starman says he does: "Red means stop. Green means go. Yellow means go very fast."

What a picture of our culture! We "go very fast" because we don't understand the purpose or the significance of life. We mistake activity for meaning and in so doing put our very lives in danger.

A few years ago I visited the British Broadcasting Corporation in London to do an interview. As I walked in, someone said to me, "By the way, there's a man who wants to see you. Peter France. Do you remember him?"

Yes, I remembered him. Peter did a program on our Mission to London in 1983. At the time he didn't believe in Jesus Christ but was searching. He filmed the program primarily because he wanted to catch us in some embarrassing comment or incident.

During one interview he told me that while studying at Oxford he had served as chairman of the Humanist Society. After graduation he moved to Hong Kong to work for Her Majesty's government.

"One day I got the Humanist Society magazine from Oxford and saw a photo of this generation's student executive committee," he said. "I was feeling very restless with my spiritual life, not believing in God, not having a purpose in life. I looked at the faces one by one, and they all seemed so empty and so lonely. And I said to myself, 'That's exactly how I've felt the last twenty years.' From then on I began to say, 'We're a bunch of empty people pretending that we know what we're talking about.'"

He told me he had begun to read some Catholic theologians. He'd even picked up the Bible. In the middle of our interview he asked, "What if I die without Jesus Christ, Luis? I've always said I'm an atheist. What about it?"

"Well, there's hell to pay, Peter," I replied.

So that's what he called the program, *Hell to Pay*. The BBC showed it on New Year's Eve several years in a row.

I didn't see him again until I walked into the BBC offices years later. By then he had grown a beard and I hardly recognized him.

"Do you remember me?" he asked.

"Yes," I said, "you're Peter France. You did a movie some years ago. I've been praying for you."

"You remembered!"

"Have you come to the Lord?"

"I *have* come to the Lord. Now I am making a series to be shown on BBC this Easter."

After years of searching, Peter France at last saw the huge difference between keeping busy and finding purpose. He'd kept extremely active as chairman of the Oxford Humanist Club, as a representative of the British government, and as a gifted television producer for the BBC. He had more activity than he could handle; what he didn't have was meaning. He found significance only when he found Jesus Christ.

I think one of the most awesome thoughts in all of the Bible is a verse in the book of Jeremiah. God says to the prophet, "I knew you before I formed you in your mother's womb. Before you were born I set you apart" (Jer. 1:5). I must have been about eighteen years old the first time I read this verse. I remember thinking, *This is amazing!*

Before my father and mother got together to do what fathers and mothers do when they want a baby, God knew all about Luis Palau. And he knew all about you too. Even if you're the result of a one-night stand. Even if your mother gave you away. Even if you were brought up in an orphanage. Even then you can say, "Lord, although I wish I'd known my dad and mom, nevertheless, you made me. I'm alive because you wanted me to be born. And God, you say in the Bible that you have a purpose for every one of us, including me."

Before egg and sperm ever came together in your mother's womb, God already knew the color of your eyes. He knew the name your parents were going to give you (whether you like your name or not). God knew what kind of floppy ears you were going to have, what sort of nose you would get, and where you were going to be born (see Ps. 139:14–15). It's awesome to realize that God knows every last thing about you!

God has a purpose and a plan for your life, whether you were born into a church-attending family or not. Whether you're Catholic or Protestant, Jewish or Muslim, atheist or agnostic. Jesus gives meaning to life because he tells us, "I knew you fully, even before you were in your mother's womb. And I have a purpose for you to fulfill, tailored to your unique personality, background, and characteristics."

Jesus also gives meaning to life by opening our eyes intellectually. That's why the Bible is so important. It's through the Bible that God teaches us about the purpose and meaning of

What Scripture helps you focus on choosing God's best?

The verse that has encouraged me most in my sense of "mission" and in choosing the high road and God's best way for me is Acts 20:24. It says, "I don't care about my own life. The most important thing is that I complete my mission, the work that the Lord Jesus gave me to tell people the good news about God's grace." That one has really helped me with my perspective.

Rebecca St. James

life. Psalm 19:7 says, "The law of the LORD is perfect, reviving the soul. The decrees of the LORD are trustworthy, making wise the simple."

You can trust the Bible 100 percent, because in it God tells us everything he wants us to know about his character, his work in the world, and our relationship to him. Scripture gives us insight and understanding about life. So read it daily!

I recommend that you use two identical editions for your Bible reading—one for reading only, the other for writing your notes and observations in the margin of the text you've just read. If you're new to reading the Bible, the *Starting Point Study Bible* will be of great help, as will the *TruthQuest Inductive Student Bible*.

Perhaps you already attend a church, yet you say, "Luis, I don't have a sense of direction. I don't have any meaning for my life. I don't understand any of this." It's not religion you need; it's Jesus Christ. Jesus offers you meaning and purpose, just as he offered it to Peter France. Don't settle for mere activity, not even activity in some church or religion. The only way to enjoy lasting significance is by settling down with Jesus Christ.

Seeks Worth vs. Enjoys Worth

A churchgoing young man from Oregon called me recently and said, "On my forehead I've always imagined one word: *loser.*" He sounded intelligent and well educated, yet he had never grasped and made a part of his personal experience the tremendous worth that Jesus Christ gives to those who belong to him.

I think millions of young people struggle with this issue. So how do they respond? Many of them pack their schedules with activity, hoping to gain a feeling of worth from a long list of accomplishments. Every day they chase after some evidence of their value—and they wind up exhausted and full of despair.

The good news of the gospel declares that we do not have to make ourselves into people of worth; we only have to grasp and live out the worth God already has given us in Jesus Christ.

What makes us into people of worth? What gives us glory? Let me suggest several biblical answers.

- *We were made in the image of God* (Gen. 1:27; James 3:9). The Bible says that unlike birds or horses or even angels, we are created in God's own image!
- *We have the capacity to create life* (Gen. 1:28). I think this is one of the most amazing gifts of God. Such power gives dignity to your sexuality and is another big reason for saving yourself sexually for marriage.

- *We have the capacity to rule over other creatures* (Gen. 1:28). God made us managers over his world.
- *We have the capacity to pray and get answers to prayer* (Phil. 4:6). It is a great mystery, but by connecting in prayer to God, you can move the hand that made the world.
- *We have the capacity to love* (1 John 3:11).
- *We have the capacity to make choices* (Josh. 24:15).
- *We can have intimate fellowship with God* (2 Cor. 13:14).

The cross of Jesus Christ reveals the greatness and meaning and significance that God intends for your life. You are so valuable to God—the Lord wants you so much in his heaven—that he gladly died for you in your place. You are *that* valuable. God would like to enjoy your company for all eternity!

"Father," Jesus prayed, "I want these whom you've given me to be with me, so they can see my glory. You gave me the glory because you loved me even before the world began!" (John 17:24). He wants us in heaven! And he wants it so badly, he said, "Here's my body. I'm coming to do your will, O God. Through my death, let these people come to heaven."

We were created for glory. We were created for grandeur and for success and for magnificence. Knowing that we are created by God gives us a sense of dignity and purpose. We were created to be respected and loved and honored and applauded. We eat it up because we were made for this.

You can lack all sorts of things—a big house, the latest clothes, an impressive family background, social connections—but through knowledge of your worth in Jesus Christ, you can move through life with dignity and confidence and great self-acceptance. I've seen tens of thousands of young people throughout the world without education, without money, who still amaze me by their obvious sense of dignity and confidence and authority.

What advice can you offer someone for selecting meaningful ways to invest time and energy?

Instead of quickly filling your calendar with commitments you are half-hearted about, first consider all your options. Choose a few opportunities that match your passions and abilities, making sure to leave a margin of time during which you can rest. This way, you'll go to your activities with energy and a sense of purpose, not dread.

Jocelyn Green, author

We do not need to desperately seek our personal worth, working hard to somehow achieve it. God invites us to acknowledge and live out the worth he already has made available to us.

Tyranny of the Urgent vs. Triumph of the Important

What rules your schedule—the urgent or the important? The two are often not the same. The urgent demands your attention, calls for your time, insists on your presence, yells for your energies—yet may not be so very important in the true scheme of things. The important, on the other hand, genuinely requires your attention, time, presence, and energies, even though it may not scream for any of them.

Consider a silly example from school life. What kind of urgent things might demand your attention, even though they can't

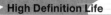

When do you feel the most significant?

When the results of my work or activity matter to someone, I feel significant. I may never find a cure for cancer or write a best-selling book. But I can use even the little opportunities God gives me to make someone else's life better or their day easier. And that makes life worth living.

Rebekah Clark, editor

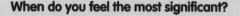

claim ultimate importance? Maybe a lunchtime rendezvous . . . an extra-credit paper in English class . . . an article for the school paper . . . an extra weight-lifting session. Any one of them might yell for your time. But are any of them vitally *important*, on par with your friends, your parents, your God?

While the noisy voices in your life may well deserve a place in your schedule, they don't necessarily belong at the top of the list, no matter how loudly they yell. We must learn not only how to tell the difference between the urgent and the important but how to choose the latter over the former.

And how do we determine the "important things"? Christians have better resources than others for making those decisions. After all, Christians not only have God's Word to guide them, they also have the Holy Spirit inside of them. Others do not.

In my opinion, everything a Christian does should be geared toward fulfilling the Great Commission (Matt. 28:18–20). Then everything that happens to you has purpose and meaning. You have lots of money? Good. Not enough money? No problem. Success in school? Fabulous. You're a well-known athlete? Great! Use your leverage to extend the kingdom.

If you understand that God has created you to help extend the kingdom of God, then everything has purpose and you don't have to despair. Life becomes tremendously exciting.

A teenager name Phil Joel also came to understand the big difference between mere activity and significance. In middle school he entered the normal "Who am I?" stage, yet his questions multiplied and intensified because he was adopted. He felt grateful for a loving family, but Phil decided he had to discover his own identity.

Phil tried to enjoy his parents' hobbies and activities, but halfway through the seventh grade, he decided, "I'm going to do the things that *I* enjoy." For one thing, that meant music. "I know it sounds stupid," he said, "but I knew—I said to myself, 'I'm going to be a professional musician.'"

That line of thought led Phil to another decision at age fourteen. Was he going to be a Christian? He knew it had to be all or nothing; it had to mean something, not just be a fun activity that he might enjoy for a while. Phil's family went to church, yet he says they believed one should "just go to church and keep it to yourself." Phil didn't feel the same way. "I knew that there needed to be more if I was going to do this whole Christianity thing," he said.

Phil's youth group attended one of our crusades in New Zealand. "I got into some trouble the week before with the long arm of the law," Phil said, "and that pushed me to start thinking, *You know what? I'm gonna make a decision one way or another in my life for who I am.*"

He had made a decision for Christ when he was eight years old, but Phil says, "I didn't know what I was doing or really if I was following Christ, or if the world was more fun or actually better than being a Christian. Did this whole Christianity stuff actually make sense?"

Phil knew the evening would come to a point when he'd have a decision to make: Did he want to follow Christ or not? Would he settle for mere activity, or would he choose significance?

"I knew that night that if Luis Palau made sense about the gospel, I was going to go for it," Phil said.

That night, Phil and a friend went forward. "I remember knowing, really knowing, that this was *it*," Phil declared. "That night was a landmark in my life. And I had to follow this Jesus, this whole Christianity bit, to the end."

Since then Phil has pursued his decision to the end. As lead vocalist and bass guitar player for the Newsboys, he now urges others all over the world to give their hearts fully to Christ. He does the same thing in his solo efforts, such as in his second project, "Bring It On." Yet he admits it's an ongoing battle.

Phil says that "Bring It On" grew out of his own dissatisfaction with a too-casual spiritual life. "I wasn't doing anything bad," he said, "but I just didn't feel like I was doing anything right, either." He'd been very active, but wondered about how much good he had really been doing. "I'd tried to play God and ask God to bless what I was doing," he said. "Now, my confidence isn't in myself so much, but in God. I wake up in the morning, and I'm jazzed to meet the Lord, to see what he's doing. It's a daily acknowledgment of God being God and me being me."[1]

God has called us not only to go to heaven when we die, not only to enjoy life, but also to partner with him in a tremendous project to reclaim this world. Together, as a global team, we proclaim the good news of Jesus Christ. Such a massive project gives purpose and meaning to life. It gives education a purpose. It gives personal connections tremendous meaning. It gives us a reason to bring home a paycheck—for something more than a cool car. Our friends, our abilities, our finances—all of them work together toward accomplishing one goal: reaching, if pos-

How did you figure out God's purpose for your life?

When my plans don't match God's, I automatically think his blueprints for my life are wrong. He doesn't really want me to do that, does he? Then opportunities and blessings pop up only because my "perfect" plans didn't work out. It turns out God really does know best.

Rebekah Clark, editor

sible, every person on the face of the earth, generation after generation, until Jesus Christ returns.

Gains Admirers vs. Attracts Colleagues

I know many young people whose nonstop activity gains them hordes of admirers. Others see their packed schedules and can't help but feel impressed. And yet that's as far as it goes. Fans may applaud, cheer, and maybe even give them an achievement award, but they remain pretty much on their own.

When you allow a divine purpose to direct your activity, however, you soon discover that God sends partners and co-workers to help you complete the assignments he gives. If you're in sync with God's heart, you see these young men and women not as competitors but as colleagues.

A man named Bob Mortimer has joined me on stage to tell audiences how God can use anybody. He grabs everyone's attention right away. You see, Bob isn't your average speaker. He's missing both legs and his left arm, yet he jokes about handicaps.

He carries a golf cap and from his wheelchair says to anyone who will listen, "You know, there really are no handicaps in this world." Then he pulls out his golf cap, puts it on, and continues. "Handicaps are up in our head. You see, I have a handy cap right here; it's a cap, and it's handy. This is the only handy cap I know. With Jesus Christ, even though you may lack three of your limbs, you're not really handicapped."

Bob may be missing three limbs, but he's still fully Bob, soul and spirit. Only his body is two-thirds gone. He's a contented, happy man who proves that Jesus Christ makes us into whole people. We don't need much body to know and serve God! I'm thrilled to be counted as one of Bob's colleagues.

Actually, I consider myself blessed to count on colleagues all over the world. A few years ago our team visited Bolivia. I had heard of a woman with a great reputation for godliness and asked her to come to the crusade. She agreed. When I asked her to pray for us, she said, "Get on your knees." We immediately fell to our knees, she laid hands on us, and then she prayed up a storm. She might be shoeless and illiterate, but that doesn't stop her from being a powerful woman of God.

In America many of us try to create our own dignity with name-brand clothes and well-put-together appearances and being seen with the right people, but it can't compare with the nobility and authority that come from walking close to God. True dignity comes from knowing that you are the handiwork of God, were rescued at the greatest price, and have a purpose filled with eternal meaning.

Great but Fallen

You and I were made for greatness, for glory, for love. You were "fearfully and wonderfully made" (Ps. 139:14 NIV) by God in your mother's womb.

So what has gone wrong? Why don't we always feel so great or lovable? If we were made to be awesome, why do we often behave so un-awesomely? If we were made for greatness, why do we so often splash around in the mud? Why do we mess up our lives when God means for those lives to be fantastic?

The answer is, we suffer from a spiritual sickness. We have a fatal flaw that only God can correct. Humankind is great but fallen. Sin has marred God's beautiful work of art. That's why we can't cure ourselves, try as we might. We all have something wrong with our hearts that requires a character transplant.

God isn't mad at us so much because we break his law but because we stupidly turn down all the amazing possibilities he offers us. He offers us life and purpose and meaning and significance, and we say, "Out of my way, God. I'd rather roll in the mud, make a fool of myself, lose my self-control, and act like an idiot."

None of us want to see ourselves as losers who deserve all the bad we get. "Yes," you may say, "I slept with my boyfriend. But I didn't really mean to do it. I'm not a bad person. I did it in a moment of weakness. But I'm not a bad person."

It's true that all of us have sinned and fallen short of the glory of God (Rom. 3:23), but that doesn't mean we're as rotten as we could possibly get. Most people I know are not downright evil. But all of us *are* weak; all of us *are* sinful. And to enjoy the greatness, glory, love, and purpose that God wants for us, we all need Jesus Christ to do for us what we cannot do ourselves.

We are great but fallen. And Jesus Christ offers us the only solution for our terrible problem. So why don't you give God a chance? God himself encourages us to discover for ourselves the truth of his Word. "I will open the windows of heaven for you," he says. "I will pour out a blessing so great you won't have enough room to take it in! Try it! Let me prove it to you!" (Mal. 3:10).

Will you let him?

HOW TO FIND Significance ACCORDING TO THE BIBLE

1. **Remember that you were created with astonishing worth.**

   "What are mortals that you should think of us, mere humans that you should care for us? For you made us only a little lower than God, and you crowned us with glory and honor" (Ps. 8:4–5).

2. **Realize that God chooses to live not in temples of stone, but within his own children.**

   "Or don't you know that your body is the temple of the Holy Spirit, who lives in you and was given to you by God?" (1 Cor. 6:19).

3. **Remember that God specially chooses every one of his children.**

   "We know that God loves you, dear brothers and sisters, and that he chose you to be his own people. For when we brought you the Good News, it was not only with words but also with power, for the Holy Spirit gave you full assurance that what we said was true" (1 Thess. 1:4–5).

4. **Consider that you—a redeemed soul—are a present from the Father to the Son.**

   [Jesus said,] "And this is the will of God, that I should not lose even one of all those he has given me, but that I should raise them to eternal life at the last day" (John 6:39).

5. **Never forget that you, along with all believers, have been given a fabulous identity.**

   "You are a chosen people. You are a kingdom of priests, God's holy nation, his very own possession. This is so you can show others the goodness of God, for he called you out of the darkness into his wonderful light" (1 Peter 2:9).

6. **Make sure you're involved in meaningful, lasting work.**

   "'But you shouldn't be so concerned about perishable things like food. Spend your energy seeking the eternal life that I, the

Son of Man, can give you. For God the Father has sent me for that very purpose.' They replied, 'What does God want us to do?' Jesus told them, 'This is what God wants you to do: Believe in the one he has sent'" (John 6:27–29).

7. **Acknowledge that God invites you to partner with him in doing great things around the world.**

   "God was in Christ, reconciling the world to himself, no longer counting people's sins against them. This is the wonderful message he has given us to tell others. We are Christ's ambassadors, and God is using us to speak to you. We urge you, as though Christ himself were here pleading with you, 'Be reconciled to God!'" (2 Cor. 5:19–20).

8. **Choose eternal rewards over short-term returns that quickly fade.**

   "Remember that in a race everyone runs, but only one person gets the prize. You also must run in such a way that you will win. All athletes practice strict self-control. They do it to win a prize that will fade away, but we do it for an eternal prize" (1 Cor. 9:24–25).

9. **Make sure your life is effective by continually evaluating your schedule.**

   "So be careful how you live, not as fools but as those who are wise. Make the most of every opportunity for doing good in these evil days" (Eph. 5:15–16).

10. **Don't allow the mistakes of your past to restrict your future.**

    "I am focusing all my energies on this one thing: Forgetting the past and looking forward to what lies ahead, I strain to reach the end of the race and receive the prize for which God, through Christ Jesus, is calling us up to heaven" (Phil. 3:13–14).

WISE WORDS

THOSE WHO HOPE
IN THE LORD
WILL RENEW
THEIR STRENGTH.
THEY WILL SOAR
ON WINGS LIKE EAGLES;
THEY WILL RUN
AND NOT GROW WEARY,
THEY WILL WALK
AND NOT BE FAINT.

the Prophet Isaiah,
Isaiah 40:31 NIV

An Anchor for the Soul

Positive Thinking or Hope?

Author Norman Cousins used to say that human beings can live for a few weeks without food, a few days without water, a few minutes without air, but not one second without hope. I think he was right. A hopeless existence just doesn't seem worth living. All of us know this almost by instinct, so we spend much of our time scouring for hope.

Sometimes in our search, however, we settle for something a little short of hope. Wanting to feel good about where we're headed, we mistake positive thinking for genuine hope.

Positive thinking is good—just not good enough. While it beats the tar out of negative thinking, nobody can hang a future on it. You can repeat cheerful sayings, look for the bright side, find silver linings, and pump yourself up all you want, but if that sums up your battle plans, you'll be staring into the darkness the moment the black clouds roll in. And positive thinking just can't help you when it's time to face that ultimate black cloud, death. The Grim Reaper doesn't smile no matter how many times you repeat the phrase, "I'm good enough, I'm smart enough, and doggone it, people like me!"

The problem with positive thinking is that it has too little power over the greatest forces that threaten us. While positive thinking can put us in the right frame of mind to tackle our problems, it can't ultimately do much about the problems themselves. If I'm sitting in the cab of a runaway truck hurtling down a mountainside, thinking positively may allow me to avoid panic and devise a last-moment escape—but if I round the bend and find the road washed out, positive thinking won't keep me from plunging to the bottom of the ravine.

Positive thinking can take us only so far. To go the rest of the way, we need hope—solid, biblical hope. So how is hope better than positive thinking? Let's consider five ways that hope outshines positive thinking and see how to go beyond positive thinking to reach genuine hope, both now and for eternity.

Positive Thinking	Hope
• Improves outlook	• Guarantees outcome
• Good at spin	• Good at regrouping
• Lessens fear	• Builds courage
• Looks for speedy change	• Counts on permanent change
• Crosses its fingers	• Bows its head

Positive thinking looks for the light at the end of the tunnel, but hope puts you in an armored truck and delivers you to the bright sunshine outside.

Improves Outlook vs. Guarantees Outcome

Positive thinking can do wonders for your outlook. When Thomas Edison tried and failed 1,000 times to find a suitable filament for his new electric lightbulb, a reporter thought he must have felt terribly discouraged over his failure. "Failure?" Edison asked. "We haven't failed. At least now we know 1,000 things that won't work." Henry Ford summed up the power of positive thinking when he said, "Whether you think you can or think you can't, you're right."

But while I'd much rather spend time with a person who thinks positively than with someone who complains all the time, I'm blessed most of all by those who express a living hope. Positive thinking may have the power to change one's outlook, but genuine hope has the power to guarantee one's destiny.

The Bible does not picture hope as mere wishful thinking, along the lines of, "Boy, I really wish it would happen, but who knows whether it ever could?" Rather, it sees hope as an expectation of future blessings that remain as yet invisible.[1] Positive thinking puts on rose-colored glasses and says, "I hope it doesn't rain this afternoon," when it knows the forecast calls for thundershowers and sprinkles already have begun to fall. Hope looks expectantly into the growing darkness and says, "I'm confident we'll be okay," even when the crops have grown waterlogged and bankruptcy looms around the corner.

The real difference between the two comes down to the source. Positive thinking flows from the human will, from the choice to believe that everything will turn out all right in the end (whether it actually does or not). Biblical hope takes its stand on the unchanging character of God, that he means what he says and that he will certainly keep all his promises (whether it looks that way or not). In other words, positive thinking depends on us, while hope depends on God.

Christians make it through even the toughest of times by the strongest hope on the planet. Those who are "in Christ" can remain confident that whatever happens to them occurs only

 words or less

Positive thinking looks for light at the end of the tunnel; hope puts you in an armored truck and delivers you to the sunshine outside.

under the watchful, loving eyes of the Lord of the universe. Because God has promised to take care of them and see that they safely reach their heavenly home, and because he has already demonstrated his faithfulness by raising Jesus Christ from the dead, Christians can live in the absolute hope that all really will be well. And that remains true even if some of us get sick with cancer, die in train wrecks, or are killed in house fires.

At this very moment history is rushing to its climax. The high point of history centers in God's Son, Jesus Christ—not only in his death on the cross for our sins, not only in his present role as our Lord, but especially in his physical return to Earth. For good reason God calls the second coming of Jesus Christ—the most frequently predicted event in the whole Bible—"the blessed hope" (Titus 2:13 NIV).

This is hope with a capital *H*! Chapter 4 of 1 Thessalonians describes how God's Son will arrive with the trumpet blast of God, the archangel will shout, and the resurrected bodies of those who have died in Jesus Christ will rise from their graves. The spirits of those who died in Jesus will return with him, and their bodies, souls, and spirits will reunite. Believers alive at that time will be instantly remade into men and women fit for heaven. The Bible says we shall all meet with the Lord in the air "and remain with him forever" (v. 17).

Why does God give us such a strange-sounding promise? The Bible tells us these things so that when our loved ones die, we will not "be full of sorrow like people who have no hope" (v. 13). With such a marvelous future, we can live in hope, even if we face cancer or catastrophe. So the Bible says, "Comfort and encourage each other with these words" (v. 18).

The tragic loss of the space shuttle *Columbia* on February 1, 2003, brought back painful memories of the first shuttle disaster almost exactly seventeen years before. I still vividly recall when the space shuttle *Challenger* exploded on January 28, 1986, just seventy-three seconds after takeoff. I'll never forget the stunned faces of those on the ground at Cape Canaveral, including the parents of teacher/astronaut Christa McAuliffe.

In the middle of that tragedy, the relatives of one doomed astronaut received a special consolation. Mission specialist Ron McNair believed in the Lord Jesus Christ, and just before he boarded the shuttle he told his family, "Jesus and I will be going up together." He had no idea that he would soon go up farther than outer space. As a shocked nation watched, Ron kept on going right up to heaven. At this very moment Ron lives beyond the stars in a place we call heaven. And one day we'll be with him again and see the Lord too.

Meanwhile, the Lord wants to keep us in suspense. He wants us to love him with overflowing happiness powered by a hope that just won't quit. As Peter said, even though we don't now see him, we believe in him and are filled with an indescribable and glorious joy (see 1 Peter 1:8).

Positive thinking may be great for improving your outlook, but to guarantee what is to come, you need solid, biblical hope.

Good at Spin vs. Good at Regrouping

You often hear about "spin" these days, about how to put the best face possible on what are often some pretty ugly situations. Positive thinkers generally make excellent spin doctors. Where you see a dilapidated house, he envisions an incredible investment opportunity. Where you notice a stain, she detects the chance to try out a new spot remover.

Now, I'm all for putting on the best face possible. Why unveil Frankenstein when you could introduce Prince Charming? "Spin" can help us see the good in something, and that's fine.

But "spin" works well only up to a certain point. Happy faces and smiling masks just can't hide the discouragement of some hurting people. They don't need "spin," they need to regroup—and that's where hope does such a fantastic job.

How do you stay hopeful in spiritually discouraging circumstances?

I remember that my spiritual hope has nothing to do with my circumstances, which are changing all the time. My hope is based on the unchanging nature of Jesus Christ, whose promises hold true no matter what. Four other ways to stay hopeful are: surround yourself with positive role models, remove the negative influences in your life, pray, and seek counseling if necessary.

Jocelyn Green, author

Solid, biblical hope not only prepares us for eternity but also helps us to function in the here and now. When the hope pouring out of God's heart energizes you, no problem or difficulty can "tap out" your inner resources. While "spin" does well at covering up embarrassing blemishes, it's not much good at providing emergency medical relief. "Spin" slaps on a new coat of paint; hope remodels the house. Hope looks straight into the face of hardship and keeps moving ahead; "spin" either tucks tail and runs or simply refuses to acknowledge the trouble.

Hope doesn't promise a life free from difficulty; it simply provides a guaranteed way through the difficulty. "I think you ought to know, dear brothers and sisters, about the trouble we went through in the province of Asia," wrote the apostle Paul to some friends. "We were crushed and completely overwhelmed, and we thought we would never live through it. In fact, we expected to die" (2 Cor. 1:8–9). Paul freely admitted that his hardships not only exceeded his coping abilities, but that the overwhelming pressure nearly choked the life out of him. And yet he persevered. How? Paul answers, "We learned not to rely on ourselves, but on God who can raise the dead. And he did deliver us from mortal danger. And we are confident that he will continue to deliver us" (2 Cor. 1:9–10).

And what gave Paul such confidence? He writes that on God "we have set our hope that he will continue to deliver us" (v. 10 NIV). No force in the universe comes near to matching the ability of godly hope to help us regroup in the face of severe challenges. Several years ago my wife, Pat, proved to me the awesome power of hope by how she faced a frightening medical challenge.

I had been in Scotland for five weeks. The last few days of our meetings Pat flew in to join me. We had planned to take time off just to relax and enjoy each other's company.

With about three days left in the campaign, she gathered herself and said, "Now, I hate to tell you this, but I think I've got a lump."

"Oh, babe," I said, "we'd better get back home and go straight to the doctor."

That's exactly what we did. I prayed that the lump would turn out to be benign; it was malignant. The specialists scheduled Pat for surgery the very next Sunday, then told her to expect two years of chemotherapy. The awful report shook us to the core. Especially me.

When we returned home from the doctor, I rushed to the basement and began to weep—not out of despair, but at the thought of all the things I hadn't done with Pat, all the places I hadn't taken her, all the ways I had fallen short as a husband. As I fled downstairs, crying and grieving, suddenly from upstairs I heard the piano playing. I listened as my wife, in a clear, soft voice, began singing some of her favorite hymns: "Under His Wings" and "The Church's One Foundation."

And I thought, *Lord, what a time to sing!* It seemed totally inappropriate.

But as the lyrics continued to drift down to the basement, carried along by Pat's confident but gentle voice, I began to change my mind. Her singing no longer seemed so out of place.

What a marvelous thing, I thought, *that a Christian can hear terrible news and still go to the piano and sing the old, affirming hymns she's known since college. To declare her love for the Lord, that her hope rests in him alone—how amazing!*

Real hope is not blind hope. Real hope can afford to be objective, to look reality in the face. The reason we have hope, the reason we avoid desperation, the reason we don't tear out our hair—no matter what comes—is that God has given us "hope as an anchor for the soul, firm and secure" (Heb. 6:19 NIV).

And that, my friend, is a long way from "spin."

Lessens Fear vs. Builds Courage

Positive thinking really can reduce some of your fears. Suppose you're camping near Crater Lake in southern Oregon.

You've enjoyed a fabulous day of hiking and sightseeing, and now it's time to retire for the evening. You snuggle into your sleeping bag, dreaming of the next day's adventure.

Suddenly you hear a snuffling among the fir trees just to the south of you. A huge shadow falls across the walls of your paper-thin tent. You grope about for a flashlight, wishing you had not recently read about one man's terrifying escape from a hungry, 800-pound bear.

At such a moment, positive thinking can do quite a lot to relieve your fear. You might remind yourself that bears generally steer clear of human campsites unless someone leaves out the groceries (and you safely stowed yours in the car trunk). Or you might tell yourself that the species *ursus* generally fears the species *homo sapiens* more than the other way around. Or you might recall that the park ranger told you earlier that he might be snooping about in your area late that evening.

On the other hand, "Late Night Snack" might be tattooed across your forehead.

In that case, you don't need positive thinking; you need courage. (A loaded gun wouldn't hurt, either.) Hope has a way of producing courage that mere positive thinking can't duplicate.

Hope builds courage in our hearts, not by denying reality but by banking on absolute certainty. When you place your hope in the trustworthy promises of God, nothing can ultimately shake you—not even death.

You can know that heaven, our future home, is an actual place, a location just as real as New York, London, Paris, or Bangkok. The Word of God says, "For we know that when this earthly tent we live in is taken down—when we die and leave these bodies—we will have a home in heaven, an eternal body made for us by God himself and not by human hands" (2 Cor. 5:1).

The Bible pictures heaven as a city, a house, a mansion, a permanent place. For the Christian, death means leaving an earthly house and moving to a heavenly house.

Heaven is the place all believers will one day call "home." Jesus referred to heaven as "my Father's house" and promised that he was going there to prepare a place for us. It's going to be beautiful. "No eye has seen, no ear has heard, and no mind has imagined what God has prepared for those who love him," the Bible declares (1 Cor. 2:9). Though we do not understand all the details, ever since Jesus Christ left this earth, he has been busily preparing a place for you and me.

On the cross, Jesus Christ purchased for us the reality of heaven. That is why he took our sins and rose from the dead—to give us the absolute assurance that we will rise from the dead, that our bodies will be lifted up from the grave, and that we will always be with the Lord

God wants all of us to join him at his house whenever it's our time to go. But we often don't get a warning.

Paul and Tiffany had no warning one Sunday afternoon when they and three school buddies took off for the afternoon. Just an hour earlier, Tiffany had joined the membership of Seaside Christian Church near her home on the Oregon coast. She wanted the world to know of her love for Jesus Christ. Her life had been good, with parents who loved her and cared for her. She excelled in track and volleyball, loved her friends, and knew they loved her. But nothing could equal that moment when she trusted Christ as her Savior.

Now she was off to celebrate that life with a group of friends. Taking off down Highway 101, loudly singing songs from the movie *Grease*, they didn't mind the sporadic rain.

Rounding a slight curve moments later, the songs abruptly died as Tiffany's friend lost control of the car. They slid across the center line and into the path of an oncoming truck, were hit, spun 360 degrees into the oncoming traffic. A van slammed into the car's left side, crushing the three teenagers in the backseat.

The next thing Paul knew, medics were strapping him onto a gurney. He didn't yet realize that his girlfriend hadn't made it.

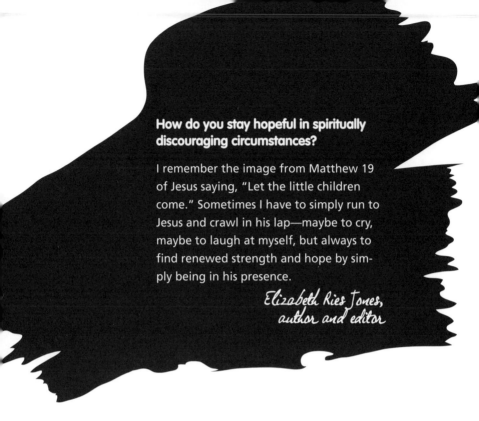

How do you stay hopeful in spiritually discouraging circumstances?

I remember the image from Matthew 19 of Jesus saying, "Let the little children come." Sometimes I have to simply run to Jesus and crawl in his lap—maybe to cry, maybe to laugh at myself, but always to find renewed strength and hope by simply being in his presence.

Elizabeth Ries Jones,
author and editor

The next morning students at Seaside High School returned to classes for the first day after Christmas break. Half an hour later, a deep silence filled the school's halls. The principal had announced Tiffany's death and the injuries of the other four friends in the car with her. Everyone knew Tiffany. Some were in band with her, others ran track or played volleyball with her. Some had worked with her on a community project, putting together food baskets for needy people. All of them had seen her smile, heard her encouraging words.

Tiffany asked questions and thought through her decisions. A few months earlier, she had attended our crusade with her boyfriend, but she didn't go forward then.

Mike Hague and Terry O'Casey, youth and senior pastors at Seaside Christian Church, helped answer some of Tiffany's questions one evening. Still, she wasn't ready to publicly commit her life to Jesus Christ.

But at the Winter Youth celebration she gave her life to God. On a Sunday morning, she was ready to tell the rest of the world. Her mother sat in the church congregation, happy to see her daughter making her statement of faith. She couldn't have known how much it would mean to her in the days and weeks that followed.

Tiffany's public statement of trust in Jesus Christ quickly traveled beyond the church walls. The services of Seaside Christian Church were videotaped and broadcast on the local cable network. The high school showed the video every day the following week. Students filled the library to hear her testimony.

God continued to use Tiffany's life to touch others' lives. At Seaside Christian Church the next Sunday morning, her best friend, Juliet, and twelve more youth and adults walked the same aisle Tiffany had walked a week earlier. They too surrendered their lives to Jesus.

Skeptics may scoff at stories like these, but let them scoff. I don't care what they say. The citizens of heaven are my friends, and the more of my friends who go there, the more I want to go myself.

That's the hope of the believer. It's a glorious hope, a real hope. Never doubt that the Lord meant what he said: "I am going to prepare a place for you" (John 14:2).

Looks for Speedy Change vs. Counts on Permanent Change

Positive thinking works best when the good times it thinks about are just around the corner. It's much harder to keep an optimistic attitude when our immediate prospects look dim. When all we have going for us is a groundless conviction that the sun will come out tomorrow, a year of overcast skies can effectively douse our enthusiasm.

On the other hand, while biblical hope never abandons the possibility that tomorrow really will bring a better day, its confidence is in eternity. It bases its hope not on human willpower but on the love of God.

The Bible bursts with story after story of how God delights to intervene in history for the benefit of his people. He loves to bring good out of evil and blessing out of catastrophe. Yet even when God chooses (for reasons known only to him) to keep us in some difficulty, he never removes our ultimate hope. An ancient prophet, Habakkuk, showed in what basket he had placed his eggs:

> Even though the fig trees have no blossoms, and there are no grapes on the vine; even though the olive crop fails, and the fields lie empty and barren; even though the flocks die in the fields, and the cattle barns are empty, yet I will rejoice in the LORD! I will be joyful in the God of my salvation. The Sovereign LORD is my strength! He will make me as surefooted as a deer and bring me safely over the mountains.
>
> Habakkuk 3:17–19

You cannot express such a strong hope without first adopting an eternal focus, something our hearts seem aware of naturally. We sense that God has "planted eternity in the human heart" (Eccles. 3:11). We know we are made not only for seventy years on Earth. We rightfully believe he wants the best for us, both now on Earth and one day in heaven.

My father died singing and clapping his hands because he knew he was about to exchange his temporary home for an eternal one. My mother told me that Dad sat up in bed, clapped his hands, and as his head fell back on the pillow, he pointed up to heaven and declared, "I'm going to be with Jesus, which is far better." A few moments later he was gone.

You seal your eternal destiny the moment you receive Jesus Christ into your heart. The Bible insists that heaven is the happy, eternal home prepared for the children of God, a place where God will wipe away every tear from our eyes. Death will be abolished forever, along with moaning and crying and pain. Just

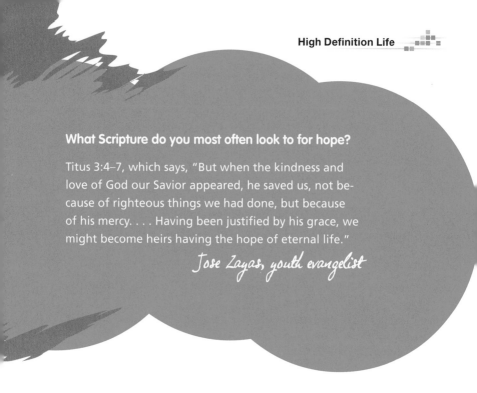

What Scripture do you most often look to for hope?

Titus 3:4–7, which says, "But when the kindness and love of God our Savior appeared, he saved us, not because of righteous things we had done, but because of his mercy. . . . Having been justified by his grace, we might become heirs having the hope of eternal life."

Jose Zayas, youth evangelist

think of it: no cancer, no AIDS, no funeral homes. No more sin, no more temptation, no more criticism, no more backstabbing, no more abuse. All of that, gone, banished for eternity.

The Bible describes heaven as a marvelous place, filled with delightful surprises. The paradise that musicians sing about, poets write about, and everyone fantasizes about is offered to us in the gospel of Jesus Christ. No one will ever be able to stop the pure and overflowing pleasure of God's children. Nonstop music and singing and praise to God will fill the air of heaven.

While eternal life begins down here the moment we receive Jesus Christ, we will enjoy it in all its dimensions when we get to heaven. The Bible declares heaven is our fantastic eternal home, better by far than any dream.

This is God's plan. This is God's desire—and every one of us can be ready for eternity when we die.

Crosses Its Fingers vs. Bows Its Head

Have you ever considered the vast number of ways we try to get an advantage on life? We cross our fingers. We knock on wood. We wish upon a falling star. We pluck four-leafed clovers. We make a wish when blowing out birthday candles.

What is all of this but an attempt to think positively? Call it superstition, call it seducing fate, but at their core all such practices are designed to boost our confidence that things really will turn out well for us.

How much better to entrust our future to the God who directs the course of the world and all things in it! Crossing one's fingers may give a little comfort, but bowing one's head in prayer can bring great confidence:

> Don't worry about anything; instead, pray about everything. Tell God what you need, and thank him for all he has done. If you do this, you will experience God's peace, which is far more wonderful than the human mind can understand. His peace will guard your hearts and minds as you live in Christ Jesus.
>
> Philippians 4:6–7

Of course, there's praying, and then there's *praying*. As a young man I used to attend a weekly all-night prayer meeting with friends. But typically I prayed with a negative attitude toward life.

Sometimes I worried about my bad habit, but I didn't know how to break the cycle. I would wake up in the morning and spend time reading the Bible, but my prayers always sounded like weeping and crying rather than joy and exuberance in the Holy Spirit. I would start out something like this: "O God, here comes another day. Lord, there are bound to be temptations. Please help me, Lord. I don't want to dishonor you. Don't let me fail you, Lord. I'm so weak. My passions are so strong. Lord, give me power. Don't let me stumble. Lord, I am so incapable. When opportunities come, please help me. Otherwise, I'm doomed to fail."

Like I said, weeping and crying.

Then, when I was about twenty-six years old, my wife and I participated in a seven-month missionary internship program. One day the instructor asked, "How do you start your day with the Lord? Do you get up and say, 'O Lord, here we go again! Darn alarm. It always seems to ring too early. It's Monday and I have to go to work again. Lord, please help me. Lord, strengthen me. Lord, don't let me lose my cool. Lord, help me make it to the five o'clock news.' Do you start with a sniveling and a pleading prayer? Or do you start with a note of praise and glory to God?"

His words struck home. I began to notice that positive believers such as the apostle Paul always began with a note of optimism and expectation: "But thanks be to God, who made us his captives and leads us along in Christ's triumphal procession," he wrote in 2 Corinthians 2:14. "Now wherever we go he uses us to tell others about the Lord and to spread the Good News like a sweet perfume."

Such an attitude stands light-years from mere positive thinking. Christian optimism is based not on human willpower but on the promises of God and on the person of Jesus Christ. The resurrected Christ lives within us. He is alive! He's almighty! He has conquered death, sin, and the devil! And therefore we can wake up in the morning with a positive outlook, no matter the circumstances.

Ray Stedman once said that 2 Corinthians 2:14 reveals "an unquenchable optimism." When you understand your rights and privileges in Jesus Christ, when you intelligently enter the spiritual Promised Land (that is, the Spirit-filled life), then you possess an unquenchable optimism.

Do you feel like a failure? Maybe you envy the kind of victories others seem to enjoy. If that describes you, then learn Paul's secret. An authentic Christian, no matter how small or large his

How do you think hope is different from positive thinking?

I can always talk myself into looking for best-case scenarios, but that doesn't mean everything will turn out happily ever after. Hope doesn't rely on my wishy-washy optimism. Hope means someone trustworthy has given me a promise that will not fail. I can look forward to its fulfillment with certainty.

Rebekah Clark, editor

or her field of work, can enjoy an unquenchable optimism, day by day. Like Paul, he or she looks to Jesus Christ and refuses to dwell on circumstances.

To be confident and effective, prayer needs to be instructed by Scripture. The more my prayer flows from the time I spend in the Word of God, the Bible, the more confidence I'll have in my requests. Why? Because my confidence will be based on the promises of God himself.

These days I get up in the morning and say, "Lord Jesus, it's a new day. I'm healthy, or at least partially so. I thank you, Lord, that I have another twenty-four hours to serve you. You are with me. You never leave me. You never forsake me. You promise to give me the words I need. You will give me discernment and wisdom. Although I will make mistakes, you can use even them to glorify yourself. What a great God you are!"

We can choose to rejoice because God lives within us. Nothing can quench our optimism. Not sickness. Not a flunked test. Not an unexpected move. Not even a plane crash.

A few years ago I met a woman who survived a horrible plane crash on the island of Tenerife, one of the worst aviation accidents in history. Two Boeing 747 jetliners collided on the runway and went up in an enormous ball of flame. Only 61 people of the 644 on board the two planes survived. This woman told me that as she saw her plane break up and a flame of fire, she cried, "Jesus, I'll see you in a few minutes!"

Despite wearing her seat belt, an explosion threw her clear of the plane, and she remembers sliding down the wing of the three-story high 747, her legs burning. For some reason she held tightly to her purse. What a silly thing, on her way to heaven with her purse! She passed out with the thought, *I'm going to heaven!*

About an hour later, she woke up, stiff and sore and lying in the grass. "Oh no!" she exclaimed, "I'm still in Tenerife!" But what impressed me most was her prayer when the plane exploded: "Jesus, I'll see you in a few minutes!"

No one and nothing can snatch a believer out of the hands of Jesus. So why *shouldn't* we go through life with an optimistic attitude, choosing to pray rather than to cross our fingers and hope for the best?

I wonder—do you have that kind of assurance? Are you certain about where you are going? If not, why not pray right now and open your heart to Jesus Christ as your Savior and Lord? Don't cross your fingers in the useless hope that somehow you might make it to heaven on your own. Ask Jesus to come into your life, to forgive your sins, to make you a child of God, and to provide you with a permanent address at his Father's house.

The Most Positive Thought of All

I doubt there's any thought quite so positive as the assurance of a permanent home in heaven. One day while visiting a family in the north of Scotland, I asked the mother, "How many children do you have?"

"Four," she replied, "three here in Scotland and one already in heaven."

How long will *you* live on Earth? Forty years? Seventy? And then where will you go? Where will you be a thousand years from this moment? For sure, none of us will be here. We are all going to be somewhere else, and there are only two possibilities. So where will you be?

Freedom is important. Food is important. Family is important. Finances are important. Having fun is important. But the question of all questions is this: *Where will you go when you die?* Do you approach the future armed only with positive thinking? Or does solid hope fill your soul?

The most dramatic event of your life will be your flight to eternity. Make your destination heaven.

HOW TO FIND Hope
ACCORDING TO THE BIBLE

1. **Adopt a positive, proactive attitude.**

   "Be strong and take courage, all you who put your hope in the LORD!" (Ps. 31:24).

2. **Focus on God's constant love for you.**

   "Let your unfailing love surround us, LORD, for our hope is in you alone" (Ps. 33:22).

3. **Discover how hope is both active (seeking) and submissive (waiting).**

   "The LORD is good to those whose hope is in him, to the one who seeks him; it is good to wait quietly for the salvation of the LORD" (Lam. 3:25–26 NIV).

4. **Immerse yourself in God's Word.**

   "Such things were written in the Scriptures long ago to teach us. They give us hope and encouragement as we wait patiently for God's promises" (Rom. 15:4).

5. **Don't be shy about asking God to intervene on your behalf.**

   "A woman who is a true widow, one who is truly alone in this world, has placed her hope in God. Night and day she asks God for help and spends much time in prayer" (1 Tim. 5:5).

6. **Watch for God's footprints in your life.**

   "But as for me, I watch in hope for the Lord, I wait for God my Savior; my God will hear me" (Micah 7:7 NIV).

7. **Remember that hope is a choice, especially when you're discouraged.**

   "Why am I discouraged? Why so sad? I will put my hope in God! I will praise him again—my Savior and my God!" (Ps. 42:11).

8. **Look at suffering as a means to strengthen your hope.**

   "We rejoice in the hope of the glory of God. Not only so, but we also rejoice in our sufferings, because we know that suffering produces perseverance; perseverance, character; and character, hope. And hope does not disappoint us, because God has poured out his love into our hearts by the Holy Spirit, whom he has given us" (Rom. 5:2–5 NIV).

9. **Reflect often on the certainty of Christ's return.**

   "Set your hope fully on the grace to be given you when Jesus Christ is revealed" (1 Peter 1:13 NIV).

10. **Recognize that God is the source of all genuine hope.**

    "Know that I am the Lord; those who hope in me will not be disappointed" (Isa. 49:23 NIV).

WISE WORDS

THIS IS WHAT
THE LORD SAYS—
YOUR REDEEMER,
THE HOLY ONE
OF ISRAEL:

"I AM THE LORD YOUR GOD,
WHO TEACHES YOU
WHAT IS BEST FOR YOU,
WHO DIRECTS YOU
IN THE WAY
YOU SHOULD GO."

Isaiah 48:17 NIV

EPILOGUE

Choose the Best

God's "best" is not like anyone else's "best." It really does stand at the top of the heap.

I've been all over the world and I've had the opportunity to sample a lot of "the best" this world has to offer. I've eaten great food. Seen great sights. Heard great speakers. Stayed in great places. Watched great performances. Enjoyed great events.

But no matter how "great" these things were, they always left a little to be desired. Maybe the steak tasted fabulous, but the room seemed too dark. Or the speaker was phenomenal, but he went on a little too long (I should talk!). Or the room was amazing, but I ran out of toilet paper. Some little thing didn't seem quite right, and despite how much I enjoyed the main event, this defect kept the experience from being all it might have been. In other words, this world's "best" depends a lot on circumstances.

But you know what? God's best doesn't.

When God promises us his best, he doesn't always mean that he'll make all our circumstances turn out just the way we think we'd like them. Instead, he means that he'll be with us completely in whatever circumstances we find ourselves—and that's why his "best" beats anything else out there by a long, long way.

Sarah Edwards reminded me of that several years ago.

I met Sarah one night in England just before we began a crusade event. Some members of our team came to me and said, "Luis, you're going to be surprised. Tonight we're having a girl give her testimony. She's twenty-one; her name is Sarah Edwards."

I looked around and saw that Sarah had already seated herself on the platform. She looked attractive and well dressed, but nothing in her appearance gave me a clue as to why she'd be speaking that night. So I approached her and said, "Sarah, I hear you're going to say something tonight?"

"Yes, sir," she replied.

"What are you going to talk about?" I asked.

"You'll find out," she said.

"Why are you here?" I wondered out loud.

"You'll find out," she repeated. She paused, smiled, then gave me one clue about her testimony. "Mr. Palau," she continued, "in the front row are my dad and mom. My dad is an atheist; he hates God, all his life he's insulted God—and now it'll be even worse because of what I'm going to say tonight."

Her statement got me really intrigued. *What is Sarah going to talk about tonight?* In a few minutes Sarah got up and moved to the podium. She seemed to walk a little wobbly but nothing too noticeable. She grabbed the podium and began to tell us what happened.

Her father had always been an enemy of God, always blaspheming God, cursing Jesus, and laughing at the Bible. He was an educated man but a mess. At fourteen years of age, Sarah

attended a camp. She listened to the gospel of Jesus and gave her heart to Christ. A few years later, when she turned eighteen, her parents sent her to Liverpool University, not far from her home.

About six months into college, she began to feel something strange in her legs. She went to see the university doctor, and after some tests the doctor said, "Sarah, this is unbelievable. You have a form of cancer that we cannot treat. We're going to have to attack your disease fast before it keeps creeping up and you lose your life while you're still in college."

So they amputated the legs of this beautiful, attractive, charming girl. When she was only eighteen and a half, surgeons cut off her legs just above the knee. You can imagine what happened with her unbelieving father! He began to curse God even more. But by then Sarah already had Christ in her heart.

The night Sarah told her story, I closely watched her dad as she described how she'd opened her heart to Christ at age fourteen.

"I know that one day when I get to heaven," she said, "God is going to give me a new pair of legs and no one will ever cut them off again. And I know something else. Because I have Jesus, I realize this life is not forever; when I go to heaven, I will *really* love life. Perhaps no guy will ever want to marry me here because I don't have these two legs. But if no man ever marries me, I don't mind that much, because Jesus is really my real friend. He is our friend."

By now her old dad was crying. I jumped up as soon as Sarah finished her testimony, and I gave an invitation. And that man who had cursed God was the first man to rise to his feet when I said, "If you want to follow Jesus, come and follow Jesus, like Sarah." He grabbed his wife, Sarah's mother, and they both came forward and gave their lives to Jesus Christ.

How's that for "best"?

No matter your circumstances, *you* can have God's best. 25 words or less

To enjoy the world's best, you want your two legs. But to enjoy God's best, it doesn't matter a whole lot whether you have them or not—you have *him,* and that makes all the difference.

Sarah knew God's best that night when her parents chose to place their faith in the God she loved so much. She might have stood on the platform a little wobbly, but I can guarantee you she felt an overwhelming joy that someone with two strong legs but no relationship with God could never experience. God's "best" really *is* best!

You know, the Lord wants the best for you. He wants to teach you what is best for you and to direct you in the way you should go. Are you listening for his voice? Are you ready to go where he directs you to go and do what he asks you to do?

Remember, that's the only way you'll ever enjoy the best of the best. No matter your circumstances, *you* can have God's best.

And you can have it starting today.

NOTES

Introduction

1. Kirsten Weir, "Second Sight: Stem Cell Surgery Returns a Teenager's Lost Eyesight," *Current Science,* October 10, 2003, http://www.findarticles.com/cf_dls/m0BFU/4_89/109082220/pl/article.jhtml.

Chapter 1: A Lifelong Source of Thrills

1. Jason Hale and Dixie-Marie Prickett, interview by Susan Stamberg, NPR.

2. Microsoft *Encarta Encyclopedia 2000,* s.v. "adrenaline rush."

3. *The Random House College Dictionary,* rev. ed., s.v. "adventure."

4. Check out www.operationworld.org for researching closed countries.

Chapter 2: A Shield All Day Long

1. Robert M. Yoder, "How Hamilcar Wilts Prepared for Everything and Got It," in *Your Own Book of Funny Stories* (New York: Pocket Books, Special Scholastic Book Services Edition, 1950), 134–36.

Chapter 3: Finding True Love

1. "What's New," Compuserve 2000, February 5, 2001.

2. Many people have asked me over the years, "How can I find 'the right one'?" There are no easy formulas to know which man or woman is "the right one" for you, but let me ask six questions.

1. *Is she or he a Christian?* The Bible says a believer should never be joined together with an unbeliever (1 Cor. 7:39; 2 Cor. 6:15). If you are a believer and the person you're dating is not a Christian, forget it. Finish it tonight. If you are interested in someone who isn't a Christian, you can pray for him or her, asking God to bring him or her to Christ—but don't start dating until you are sure he or she belongs to God.

2. *Am I proud of him or her?* If you're embarrassed to introduce your boyfriend to your friends or family, something is wrong. In a healthy couple, the husband praises his wife (Prov. 31:28). True love praises the beloved. It doesn't consider him or her inferior.

3. *Am I jealous or suspicious of him or her without good reason?* It's a bad sign when you don't want your girlfriend to talk to any other guy or your boyfriend to talk to any other girl. Jealousy is a sick attitude of the heart that's always suspicious, always wondering, and never content or at rest. Love isn't like that.

4. *Do I respect her or him?* The Bible says love does not act improperly (1 Cor. 13:4–7). Love is pure. So when your boyfriend or girlfriend insists on too much touchin' and squeezin', watch out. Do you take liberties in handling him or her? When the passion is gone, so is the so-called love.

   And ladies, if your boyfriend mistreats you when you're dating, you can bet he'll get worse once you're married.

5. *When I pray about marriage, do I have peace in my heart or confusion?* Never even think about marrying someone without first praying about it for many hours. Get on your knees every week and spend significant time with God. Read the Bible; think about it; make notes in a notebook. Seek the mind of God. If you marry flippantly, you'll suffer.

   Also look for counsel from Christian couples who obviously love each other, who really get along. Ask for their advice. Don't make this decision on your own.

6. *Are we suited for each other?* The Bible says you need a partner suitable for you (Gen. 2:18). Do you fit each other? Often an outgoing person marries a quiet person, while a hard-nosed person marries a flexible person. Opposites really do attract.

You need to ask yourself, "Is this God's woman for me? Is this God's man for me? Are we going to get along at every level?" Not just, "Do I like her eyes and all the kissing stuff?" Not only, "Do I like his body, his looks, his car?" Those things are important but very secondary. Make sure you emphasize the crucial.

Chapter 4: A Friend Who Sticks Closer Than a Brother

1. Suzanne Kerins, "Lonely Robbie's Torment," Sunday Mirror.co.uk, May 16, 2004. http://www.sundaymirror.co.uk/news/tm_objectid=14244400&method=full&siteid106694&headline=lonely-robbie-s-torment-name_page.html.

Chapter 5: A Winner at the Game of Life

1. John Piper, *Desiring God,* 10th ann. expanded ed. (Sisters, OR: Multnomah Books, 1996), 162.

2. David G. Myers, *The American Paradox: Spiritual Hunger in an Age of Plenty* (New Haven, CT: Yale University Press, 2000), quoted in Dr. Joyce Brothers, "You Can Lead a More Joyful Life," *Parade,* October 15, 2000, 6.

3. "Finding a Faith—and a Wife," *The Door,* December 1992, 2.

4. Mark Twain, quoted in Jon Winokur, ed., *The Portable Curmudgeon* (New York: New American Library, 1987), 97.

5. Marlo Thomas, quoted in Robert Byrne, *1,911 Best Things Anybody Ever Said* (New York: Fawcett Columbine, 1988), 171.

6. Jessica McBride, "Eagle Scout Is Murder Suspect," *Milwaukee Journal* Sentinel, February 7, 2004, http://www.jsonline.com/news/state/feb04/205991.asp?source=tmj4.

Chapter 6: A Festival in Your Heart

1. Brothers, "A More Joyful Life," 6.

2. Quoted in Nancy Haught, "Mind-Set/Satisfaction: Tough Life Experiences Led Columnist-Novelist Anna Quindlen to Be Awake to the World and Not Miss Happiness," *The Sunday Oregonian*, October 22, 2000, L11.

3. Hannah Whitall Smith, *The God of All Comfort* (Westwood, NJ: Christian Library, 1984), 7.

4. Piper, *Desiring God*, 34.

5. See *Say Yes: How to Renew Your Spiritual Passion* by Luis Palau (Grand Rapids: Discovery House , 1995) for a full meaning of "an overflowing cup" and "the fullness of the Holy Spirit," or request an excerpt by writing to me at palau@palau.org.

6. Brothers, "A More Joyful Life," 6.

7. Merrill C. Tenney, ed., *The Zondervan Pictorial Encyclopedia of the Bible*, vol 3 (Grand Rapids: Zondervan, 1975), 714.

8. Write to me at palau@palau.org to request a copy of my article, "Planting Your Roots Deeply into the Local Church."

Chapter 7: A Priceless Gift That Costs Us Nothing

1. Quoted in Byrne, *1,911 Best Things Anybody Ever Said*, 393.

2. Associated Press, "Missionary Whose Wife, Daughter Perished in Peru Lays Trust in God," *Holland Sentinel*, July 5, 2001, http://www.hollandsentinel.com/stories/070501/new_0705010033.shtml.

3. Paul Williams, "Peace: Will It Ever Happen to Me?" St. James Churches, 2001. www.saintjames.org.uk/sermons/peace.htm.

Chapter 8: A Fresh Start

1. Dr. Robert Wallace, "Teen Is Taking a Hard Step in Forgiveness," *Holland Sentinel*, April 10, 2004, http://www.hollandsentinel.com/stories/041004/fea_041004058.shtml.

Chapter 9: A Sense of Destiny

1. "Phil Joel, Biography," http://www.christianitytoday.com/music/artists/philjoel.html.

Chapter 10: An Anchor for the Soul

1. *The New Bible Dictionary, 2d ed.*, ed. J. D. Douglas, F. F. Bruce, et al. (Wheaton: Tyndale, 1962), s.v. "hope."

Correspondence Information

Thank you for reading this book! Every reader's experience with a particular book is different. So I hope I hear from you about what you found helpful, insightful, or thought-provoking. I also invite you to send me your specific questions or concerns—or tell me if you disagree with something I've said. That's okay too!

Here's how to reach me:

Luis Palau
P.O. Box 1173
Portland, OR 97207
telephone (503) 614-1500
fax (503) 614-1599
palau@palau.org
www.palau.org

Free Online Offers

You'll find free excerpts from my other books at www.palau.org.

While you're online, please take a minute to sign our www.palau.org guest book and read what other readers have to say about *High Definition Life*. Then please feel free to add your own comments on our "Readers Say" page. You'll also find online discounts if you want to obtain another copy of this book for a relative or friend.

Also be sure to check out the online version of our daily "Reaching Your World with Luis Palau" two-minute radio program. You'll find a link right off our www.palau.org home page. There you can sign up to receive our free weekly "Healthy Habits for Spiritual Growth" devotional e-zine.

All of these resources are designed to encourage and inspire your faith.

God richly bless you in every area of your life as you seek his best!

Luis Palau is an internationally known evangelist and speaker and the author of numerous books, including *God Is Relevant, Where Is God When Bad Things Happen?* and *It's a God Thing.* Well-known for his successful festival evangelism ministry, he now sponsors and speaks at six major festivals in the United States and abroad every year. Palau's ministry is based in Portland, Oregon, but his evangelistic outreach is global.

Steve Halliday is president of Crown Media, Ltd., a literary company that specializes in book editing and collaboration. He and his wife, Lisa, live in Portland, Oregon.